W9-BNN-740

8 ways to tell your fortune

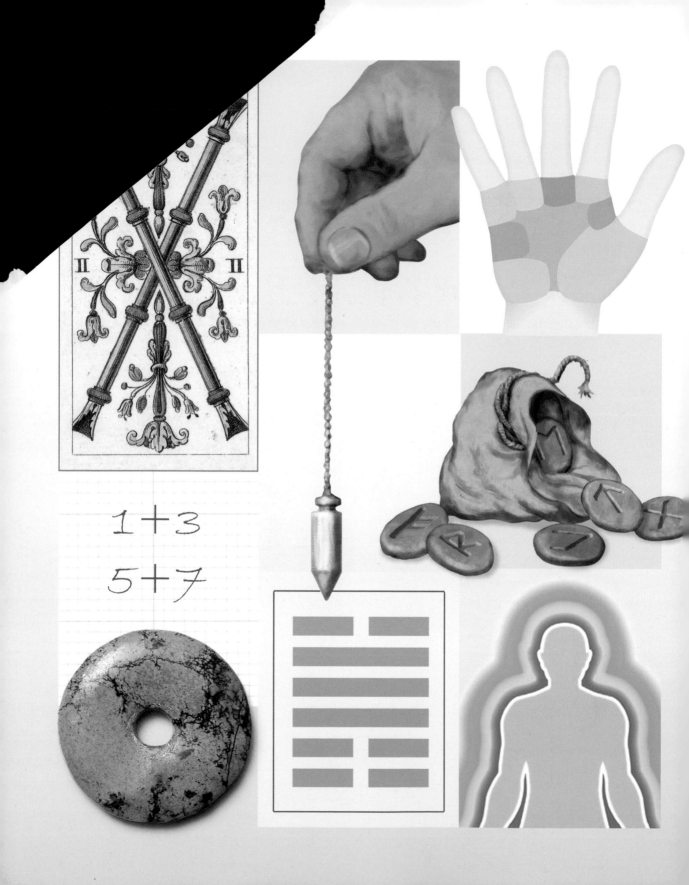

8 ways to tell your fortune

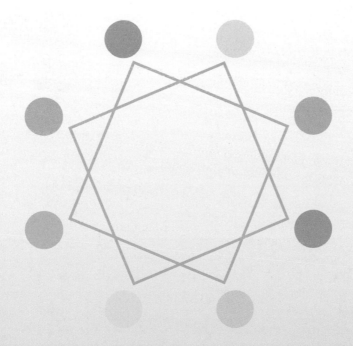

Sarah Bartlett

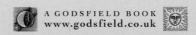

A GODSFIELD BOOK
www.godsfield.co.uk

An Hachette Livre UK Company

First published in Great Britain in 2006 by Godsfield Press
a division of Octopus Publishing Group Ltd
2–4 Heron Quays, London E14 4JP

Copyright © Octopus Publishing Group 2006
Text copyright © Sarah Bartlett 2006

Distributed in the United States and Canada by
Sterling Publishing Co., Inc.
387 Park Avenue South, New York, NY 10016-8810

Sarah Bartlett asserts the moral right to be identified as
the author of this work.

All rights reserved. No part of this work may be reproduced
or utilized in any form or by any means, electronic or
mechanical, including photocopying, recording or by any
information storage and retrieval system, without the prior
written permission of the publisher.

ISBN-13: 978-1-84181-301-1
ISBN-10: 1-84181-301-X

A CIP catalogue record for this book is available from the
British Library

Printed and bound in China

10 9 8 7 6 5 4 3

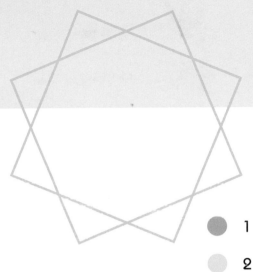

Contents

Introduction

This practical book presents eight simple techniques that anyone can use to access their intuition, aid decision-making and foretell the future. These methods, drawn from cultures all over the world, have stood the test of time as reliable ways of providing life guidance.

Using divination to guide your life

Divination, or fortune-telling, is not a science that can be measured, but an art that adapts to your individual needs. Its aim is to acquire knowledge of the past, the present and, primarily, the future, by developing your own intuition and insight. It involves using time-honoured tools of the trade, such as the Tarot and runes – and all the other fortune-telling methods described in this book – to get in touch with the untapped source of power that is hidden deep within you. This is your direct link to a universal energy drawn from all humankind in the past, present and future.

You may already have access to some intuitive channels. How often do you instinctively 'feel' that something is going to happen, or 'know' who is about to call you on the phone? This kind of premonition is common in many people, and means that you are unconsciously connecting with the deepest levels of information within yourself. Divination gets you immediately in touch with these unconscious pathways. It gives you access to the unknown powers within you, which can guide you in making decisions and herald the way to clarity of thinking and purpose, as well as predicting the outcome of any issue or question that you have raised. Treat divination with an open mind and mostly an open heart. Work and play with the ideas revealed here, and enjoy discovering how to create your own good fortune.

The Roman goddess Fortuna bestows a beggar with good luck.

A fortune-teller begins a reading by laying out the Tarot cards in particular pattern.

The origins of fortune-telling

The word 'fortune' is rooted in the Latin word *fortuna*, meaning 'luck'. This can imply good or bad luck, good or bad fortune. However, human nature being what it is, everyone wants good luck and good fortune. This book guides you in developing your own ability to make conscious choices, based on what is 'good' for your life journey, and in turning negative feelings, worries or fears into positive luck.

The Roman goddess Fortuna was the personification of luck. She was worshipped under various titles, including Fortuna Annonaria (for a good harvest) and Fortuna Virilis (to bring good fortune to a man's career). But not all her emanations were positive: she could be Fortuna Dubia (doubtful), Fortuna Mala (plain bad luck) or Fortuna Brevis (fickle fortune).

Fortune-telling was popularized in the 18th century, when it evolved as a curiosity parlour game. Family and friends would dress up in 'gypsy' clothes and read each other's palms or fortune in the cards. In the early 20th century this kind of fortune-telling

Crystals connect you to universal vibrations.

became distinct from 'divination', due to the social prejudices of the times. Elite occultist groups despised fortune-tellers, who were seen as phoneys or frauds, making easy money out of naive women and the lower classes.

Personal fortune-telling is simply a way to find out the kind of luck you have right now, and the kind you will have in the future. By making your own decisions, with greater insights into self-awareness, you can create the right kind of fortune in your life.

I Ching hexagram reveals your destiny.

By understanding the current patterns and rhythms at work, regarding a particular issue, you can work *with* the energy rather than battling naively against it.

The benefits of divination

Much more than an entertaining party game, personal fortune-telling is a time-honoured way of accessing your deepest knowledge. The techniques in this book can help you look into the future to increase your self-knowledge, ease decision-making and plan for greater success and happiness. You will learn:

- How a morning Tarot reading can help you focus on the day's most important tasks.
- What your name and birth date reveal about your personal destiny.
- How to explore what the different aspects of your hand reveal about your future relationships, career, talents and temperament.
- How to make your own set of runes and use them to answer questions and make decisions.
- What the colours in your aura show about your secret desires.
- How to use a pendulum to help you make the right decisions.
- How the I Ching oracle can help you make important life changes.
- How your zodiac crystal can point the way to a happy future.

How to use this book

There are eight basic methods of fortune-telling described in this book. Each chapter is self-contained, but eventually you can combine several methods of divination, or concentrate solely on one. There may be one technique that instantly attracts you, so don't feel that you have to start with Tarot and finish with the crystal zodiac, following strictly the order of the chapters.

No one technique is more difficult than any other – it's all a matter of which one suits you. Do try them all, though, and you will soon realize that some techniques you will find easy and seem to become second nature, while others require more practice and understanding. Often it's the latter techniques that are ultimately more enlightening and satisfying, once you have mastered them.

Above all, trust in yourself: take control of your destiny, and good fortune will be yours.

Practical spreads show you how to put your knowledge into practice. Step-by-step guidelines help you to work easily with the technique and to get you in touch with your own intuition.

The introduction gives you an overview of the history and benefits of each specific technique along with various methods that have been traditionally used. It tells you what each fortune-telling tool can reveal about your future.

Directory spreads reveal the secret information of each specific fortune-telling tool. Each card, rune, crystal or I Ching hexagram has it's own unique interpretation, and these are easy to refer to as soon as you start using the practical information.

TAROT

1 • TAROT

As long as you don't deny responsibility for your choices, the Tarot can reveal past, present and future behaviour. When you start practising with a Tarot card for the day, you will soon see how it corresponds to the energy, experiences and events over the following 24 hours.

What can the Tarot reveal about your future?

The Tarot reveals your future potential – it's rather like looking in a mirror. First it tells you about your current hopes, dreams or aspirations, and what you project into the future. Then it tells you about the outcome of your choices. You can discover the direction in which you're going and what to do about it; how to improve your lifestyle, love life or personal goals; and how to generally develop your own ability to make decisions and the right choices.

The Tarot is an objective mirror. The invaluable benefit of this kind of divination is that you can't cheat – and the cards never lie.

The benefits of using the Tarot

- Instantly tap into what you truly want or need in life.
- Find out what your partner feels about you.
- Discover your potential for the future.
- Reveal the outcome of a current situation.
- Discover a unique tool for self-understanding.
- Know the next steps of your personal journey.

Tarot history

The Tarot is a deck of 78 mystical cards. It has been one of the most important Western mystical pathways for hundreds of years. With connections to alchemy,

psychology, astrology, numerology, cabbala, Christian mysticism, Eastern philosophy and many other esoteric traditions, the Tarot is available to everyone.

Decks of mystical numbered cards have long existed in India and the East, and were probably brought back to Europe by the Knights Templar during and after the Crusades in the Holy Land. There have also been suggestions that travelling gypsies from Egypt brought the Tarot to Europe.

Most sources state that the first Tarot decks appeared in the early 14th century, arising from a combination of Italian playing cards, with their four suits, and the curious and far more mysterious set of 22 Major Arcana cards, whose origin still remains shrouded in mystery.

The Tarot pack and how to use it

The Tarot deck is made up of the 22 cards of the Major Arcana, plus a further four suits of 14 cards each, known as the Minor Arcana. The four suits are each numbered from Ace through to Ten, but differ from normal playing cards because there are four court cards: the Page, Knight, Queen and King. If you are a beginner, use the 22 Major Arcana cards on their own first. These are very potent symbols and are easy to get to know.

Always read Tarot cards in a quiet place. Focus clearly on what you want to know; light candles, burn incense or have soothing music playing in the background to enhance the atmosphere. But don't try to do too many readings in one day about the same issue, for this will only confuse you.

Tarot tips

Nowadays there are many special Tarot packs, associated with anything from gnomes to rock'n'roll – it's all a question of personal taste. Opt for one of the traditional packs, such as the Rider Waite or Universal decks, where the pictorial images are easier to understand.

Caring for your pack

There are no specific rules about looking after your Tarot cards, but treat them as you would your friends. When you first take them out of their box, place them on a clean table and allow them to 'breathe', both exuding their own energy and taking in yours.

Connect with the cards: touch them, pick them up, study them. Take your time and, once you have used them, either return them to their box or wrap a silk scarf around them, to protect them from inauspicious energy and harmful sunlight.

Shuffling the cards

Shuffling is simply a process to make the choice of card as random as possible. While you're shuffling the deck, concentrate on the specific issue or question you have in mind. If you can't shuffle the cards like a deck of normal playing cards, in your hands, spread them out face-down on a table or on the floor and swirl them around in a circle, until you feel intuitively that the cards are ready to be drawn together into a pile. You can cut the cards a few times afterwards, as a final flourish.

Drawing the cards

Place the pack face-down on the table or floor, then draw it gradually to the left or right until you have made a long line of overlapping cards. Keep focusing on your question or issue all the time. When you feel ready, slowly run your fingers along the cards and stop when you sense that a card seems literally to be asking you to pick it. You can also close your eyes, while still focusing on your question or issue.

Reversed cards

There is a lot of debate about reversed cards — that is, cards that are drawn or laid out facing you with the picture upside-down. If you're a beginner, I suggest that you don't worry about reversed meanings, or think of them as being negative. Turn the cards the right way up – they will reveal just as much as you need to know.

Reading for yourself

Always try to be objective. It's very easy to see what you want to see, when you are reading Tarot cards for yourself. But the cards never lie – it's only people who do that! So check the interpretations, and work with the ideas in relation to your specific question or issue. This book isn't large enough to give you complete interpretations for all the Minor Arcana cards (although keywords are given on pages 28–31), so work with the Major Arcana first, to get to know what they mean.

Throughout the card interpretations I refer to 'past', 'future', 'outcome' and 'you now' positions. This is because in the spreads that follow (see pages 32–37) there will often be one card that represents the past, one that represents the future, one that represents the outcome and one that represents you now, or your current situation.

The Major Arcana

The 22 Major Arcana cards represent the most profound, and yet the most simple, of symbols. 'Arcana' means secrets, and an Arca was a deep chest or box. As you use the cards, imagine that you're reaching down into the bottom of the chest for its hidden secrets.

How to interpret the cards

The following interpretations for each card in the Major Arcana will give you lots to go on, but it's your own interpretation that matters. Look at each card in turn and decide first whether you like it, hate it or feel indifferent about it. Jot down notes about those feelings and then check the meanings of the cards and see which are relevant to your life.

Each Tarot card has several keywords/phrases listed on pages 17–27, for quick interpretation.

The 22 Major Arcana cards are numbered from 1 to 21, plus The Fool, which has no number, but is sometimes referred to as 0.

Getting to know the Major Arcana

Every morning pick one Major Arcana card to see what kind of day you can expect, what sort of tasks you may need to perform or who is going to come into your life. Later on, decide what the card actually referred to. Did it have relevance in a different way from what it immediately suggested or in the way you interpreted it initially?

Separate the Major cards from the others. Check your response to each card in turn as you look at them. Which do you like, which do you hate or fear? Work first with the images and interpretations for those that stand out in this way. If you want to consult the Tarot to confirm your feelings or instincts about a situation, you can simply draw one card without doing a spread. Look up the card's interpretation and relate it to the situation in question.

IL MATTO

IL BAGATTEL.

The Fool
Unnumbered

Keywords/phrases Impulsiveness, infatuation, blindness to the truth, childlike, pure and uncorrupt, ready to leap into anything and take each adventure as it comes, the eternal optimist
Interpretations The Fool usually implies new beginnings and a childlike enthusiasm for life. Watch out for falling in love with love and not looking where a relationship is heading. This card implies that you have an immature attitude towards relationships or professional abilities. The Fool can mean that you won't listen to anyone's advice, and that you are careless with promises and feelings. You may be blind to future heartache or rush into a new venture too soon, without thinking things through. Look before you leap.

The Magician
Arcanum 1

Keywords/phrases Initiative, persuasion; wisdom is the key to success, but don't deceive yourself that you know all the answers
Interpretations Adapt to changing circumstances, juggle with ideas and find the right way forward – it's time to be flexible. You might have to guide a friend or partner towards making the right choice for themselves. Persuasion is your friend, so set the pace and inspire others with your ideas. This is a 'go out and get it' card. As a future card, it reveals that you will soon have to prove that you can communicate effectively.

The High Priestess
Arcanum 2

Keywords/phrases Secrets, hidden feelings, intuition, the healer, feminine power

Interpretations This card indicates that you fear finding out how you really feel about someone. It's time to develop your awareness and use your intuition concerning what you really want and where you are going. There are many secrets in your heart and if you learn to look within you will find the truth. Maybe you are finding it hard to communicate your feelings to someone? As an outcome card, The High Priestess indicates that you will soon be enlightened about a problem or that a secret will be revealed.

The Empress
Arcanum 3

Keywords/phrases Action, development, feminine wisdom and vitality, sensual pleasure

Interpretations You can be assured of progress in any plan, however daunting it may seem. If you have asked a question about relationships, The Empress indicates that you might have to motivate your partner or mother him or her. It can also suggest that there is a disruptive female influence in your life. Material wealth or property will be important to you in the future; but it's also time to be creative with your life, rather than assume things will just fall into your lap. The Empress reveals that you must feel, as well as think, your way through life.

The Emperor
Arcanum 4

Keywords/phrases Power, authority, father figure; leadership and the power of reason, insensitivity in feeling towards others, passion, assertiveness

Interpretations This card represents a male influence, and in a question concerning partnership it signifies that you have the will, and the need, to take control of the relationship. It's time to keep personal feelings out of the firing line and base your decisions on pure fact. As a future card, it means that you will be attracted to a strong, dominating person or a successful career go-getter. Power-trippers and cold-hearted lovers are also indicated, who may be reliable around the office or in bed, but you will never know their true motives.

The Hierophant
Arcanum 5

Keywords/phrases Conforming, holding back, respect, teaching, traditional rules and ceremony

Interpretations If in a 'you now' position, this means that you are stuck in your ways and unwilling to adapt to others. Clinging to the past means that you can't move on and accept the necessary changes that will improve your life. The Hierophant often represents a specific person whom you will meet in the future: someone who can offer you good advice, or a guru, spiritual adviser or teacher who should be trusted. It also implies meeting someone you feel you've known before and with whom you have an immediate rapport. But however much you may trust your own beliefs, there are others who have their own agenda.

The Lovers
Arcanum 6

Keywords/phrases Love, completeness, choice, temptation, commitment, the power of love and how you deal with it

Interpretations Your heart rules your head and new romance could come into your life without you even looking for it. This card also implies that it's time to make a relationship choice. Do you commit? Will your partner commit? Do you go your own ways? Conflicts can be resolved if this card is in the future position, but it can also indicate that temptation will test the strength of a current relationship. Love triangles are also indicated by this card in a future position, or having to choose between two people. The Lovers ask you to think about what you mean by love and to take responsibility for your choices.

The Chariot
Arcanum 7

Keywords/phrases Diligence, will power, honesty, perseverance, control over your feelings and thoughts, being pulled in two directions and learning to stick to the right path

Interpretations There may be conflicting influences in your life, but you have now reached a point where you can stand up for your own beliefs and make decisions based on what you want, rather than what other people assume is right for you. You can achieve success in any enterprise and overcome all obstacles in your way. As a future card, The Chariot indicates that timing and control are essential to get what you want, so don't let the reins slip through your fingers: stay on top. Maybe your relationship needs re-evaluating? Whatever your mission, only *you* can make it work.

Justice
Arcanum 8

Keywords/phrases Fairness, harmony, equality, objective thoughts and balanced relationships are favoured, interaction and communication are essential

Interpretations You may find this card turning up when a decision needs to be made and you will then be able to do so with a more rational viewpoint than before. As a past card, Justice implies that you've got what you deserve and things are set to improve. Whatever the results of a series of events, things will now work out for you. Legal issues and settlements are often indicated by this card in a future position, which implies they will have a successful outcome.

The Hermit
Arcanum 9

Keywords/phrases Discrimination, discretion, detachment, withdrawal, the search for inner wisdom, knowledge is a burden, fear of revealing a secret

Interpretations Reflect carefully before you make a choice, and avoid rushing ahead with plans that could push others into doing something against their better judgement. If it's a relationship issue, think long and hard before committing yourself. As a past card, The Hermit shows that you may have chosen to forget certain facts or are refusing to face up to the truth. As a future card, it shows that you will have to put your plans on hold until you can discriminate between what is right for you and what isn't.

The Wheel of Fortune

Arcanum 10

Keywords/phrases Inevitability, luck, timing, there is no certainty in life except uncertainty, each moment is a new beginning, the only constancy is change itself

Interpretations Whatever is happening, a new phase in your life is now beginning, whether or not you want it to. Don't fear change; instead, embrace it for future happiness. The Wheel can signify infatuation or a new romance, escaping from a difficult relationship or improving an existing one. It's time for you to jump on the wagon and take the chances that are coming your way. Unexpected events will give you the motivation to change your life for the better.

Strength

Arcanum 11

Keywords/phrases Courage, self-awareness, personal power, facing up to reality, taking control of your life, learning to take responsibility for your actions

Interpretations Strength and the courage of your convictions are needed now. Be prepared to face any threat with determination. If this card is in the 'you now' position, it's time to force an issue in order to achieve results. If you are asking a question concerning love or romance, are you giving too much of yourself, or not getting anything back from a partner? If Strength is in a future position, self-awareness and courage will bring you success.

The Hanged Man

Arcanum 12

Keywords/phrases Transition, readjustment, limbo, sacrifice may be necessary, boredom with life, anticipation of progress, static relationships

Interpretations In a 'you now' position, this card means that you are at a crossroads and may have to stand back and look carefully at all the issues involved, or simply get out of a rut. You are in limbo about what you want to do next, or are going through a ceasefire in a relationship clash. The Hanged Man also warns you about making sacrifices. Fine, if you are ready to give up a bad influence in your life, but think clearly about whether you are being manipulated by others. As a future card, The Hanged Man indicates that you will undergo a change of mind and that readjustment about your feelings will be necessary to forge ahead with your plans.

Death

Arcanum 13

Keywords/phrases Change, new beginnings, transformation, the end of an old cycle and beginning of a new one, letting go of old values, don't fear becoming true to yourself

Interpretations This card often spooks people, but don't take it literally. Death simply implies that something has reached the end of a cycle. It could be a love affair, a job or a belief system that now needs to be expressed or changed. When in the 'you now' position, Death can imply that you are in the process of changing your life, but are perhaps concerned about the consequences. In the future position, it relates to imminent change that will bring vitality and a completely new you.

Temperance

Arcanum 14

Keywords/phrases Self-control, compromise, moderation, virtue, the blending of ideas, harmony and understanding

Interpretations Whenever you draw this card, good management of your relationships is in progress. There is harmony between your desires and your needs, and you are mentally and emotionally in balance. If you're trying to make a decision, you will find a solution and it will be much easier to see another person's point of view. As a 'you now' card, Temperance signifies that your self-control and willingness to compromise are a good influence on others. As a future card, it shows that you may have to moderate your desires and try to see both sides of an argument. But clarification of your true goals or aspirations is coming your way.

The Devil

Arcanum 15

Keywords/phrases Illusion, sexual temptation, materialism, thirst for money or power, unconscious reactions, childlike responses

Interpretations When this card is in the 'you now' position, it can simply mean that you are attracted to someone for lust or money. Or you are getting involved in a relationship and are confusing sexual desire with love. As a future card, The Devil indicates that you are going to have to fight against the temptations of materialism or power, and take care not to be led astray by someone who wants to take control over you or assert their power. Sometimes this card reveals that you are acting like a child, without awareness of your actions or the consequences.

The Tower
Arcanum 16

Keywords/phrases External disruption, unexpected events, breakdown of the old to herald the new, acceptance that no defence is totally secure, learning to adapt and adjust

Interpretations There is, or will be, change in an unexpected and external manner when this card appears in a spread. It seems as if it's fated and that you are not responsible. The Tower reveals that there is a catalyst or outside influence that comes into your life to instigate these changes. It may be a person or a set of circumstances over which you have no control. It can feel either liberating or uncomfortable, but you now have the necessary strength to adapt and move on. This card asks you to welcome new challenges, rather than avoid them.

The Star
Arcanum 17

Keywords/phrases Inspiration, ideal love, truth revealed, realization of a dream, insight and self-belief are essential for happiness

Interpretations This card is all about having an optimistic attitude. If you really believe and trust in yourself, you can create your own opportunities. The Star is beneficial in any spread and indicates success in love, work or financial aspirations. As a future card, it reveals that a revelation is about to come to you in the nicest possible way. The only downside of this card is when it's in the blockage position and indicates that your expectations are so high that no one – not even yourself – can live up to them right now.

The Moon
Arcanum 18

Keywords/phrases Intuition, emotion, self-deceit, warning, a tricky love affair, blindness to the truth, unrealistic dreams

Interpretations This is a complex card because its very nature is deceptive. So always interpret The Moon first as a warning that things may not be all they seem. Perhaps you are wrong, your judgement is unsound or someone is taking advantage of you? Try to tap into your intuition rather than your imagination – they're very different. As a future card, The Moon signifies that someone will be dishonest: either you or a partner or friend. It also indicates that you're so wrapped up in your emotions and feelings that you don't have a clear, rational view of the truth of a matter.

The Sun
Arcanum 19

Keywords/phrases Communication, sharing, happiness, joy, positive energy, creativity, growth, accomplishment in love, new friendship

Interpretations As a 'you now' card, The Sun shows that it's time to communicate your feelings and express your dreams. This is a positive card and always signifies success and happiness. You can now accept your friends or partner for who they are and vice versa. As a future card, it indicates that you can expect to be happier, more fun-loving and liberated from past doubts and fears. A fulfilling relationship (not necessarily an intimate one) will begin and will have a positive effect on your life. As a blockage card, The Sun signifies that you may be exaggerating how happy you are, or only looking at the surface of a relationship.

Judgement
Arcanum 20

Keywords/phrases Liberation, atonement, transformation, accounting for past actions, re-evaluation and revival, dropping old values, embracing new ones; accepting things the way they are – there is no one to blame, not even yourself

Interpretations Judgement implies that you are now liberating yourself from old attitudes – whether towards a lover, your family or patterns of behaviour that haven't been right for you. You have new insights into how to handle your relationships. This is your chance to start afresh, let go of the past and stop feeling guilty for your actions. As a future card, Judgement shows that you will have to make a decision by facing the facts, rather than avoiding them.

The World
Arcanum 21

Keywords/phrases Completion, fulfilment, freedom, cosmic love, freedom from fear, reward for hard work and effort, time for celebration of yourself and others

Interpretations A positive card in any spread, The World means that you are coming to terms with yourself, your sense of individual value and the way you relate to others. It can also mean that you've met the ultimate partner or found the perfect vocation, and there's no turning back. As a future card, it indicates that you can look forward to success in relationships and all creative enterprises. Sometimes this card is interpreted as meaning 'The world is yours'. You're about to embark on the trip of a lifetime – whether literally or on a new venture.

The Minor Arcana

The Minor Arcana consist of four suits – Wands, Cups, Swords and Pentacles – which are very similar to those of a normal playing-card deck, except that there are four court cards, the Page, Knight, Queen and King. Here are keyword interpretations for each card.

Minor Arcana keyword interpretations

WANDS

Ace of Wands
Enterprise, creativity

Two of Wands
Adventure, inspiration

Three of Wands
Deliberation, aspiration

Four of Wands
Prosperity, completion
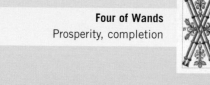

Five of Wands
Competition, challenge

Six of Wands
Self-confidence, good news

Seven of Wands
Perseverance, gain

Eight of Wands
Modification of plans

Nine of Wands
Strength to face challenges

Ten of Wands
Self-imposed limitations

Page of Wands
Daring, energy, a younger admirer

Knight of Wands
Adventure, risk, a new lover

Queen of Wands
Creative success, a woman of vision

King of Wands
Loyalty, an honest man

CUPS

Ace of Cups
Love, joy, fertility

Eight of Cups
Retreat, decline of love, moving on

Two of Cups
Romance, clarity, sexual union

Nine of Cups
Contentment, complacency

Three of Cups
Celebration, abundance

Ten of Cups
Emotional happiness, success

Four of Cups
Sensitivity, seduction

Page of Cups
A sensitive man, a new relationship

Five of Cups
Emotional imbalance, disillusionment

Knight of Cups
A messenger, an invitation to love

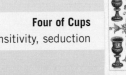

Six of Cups
Nostalgia, good memories

Queen of Cups
Emotional integrity, a woman of grace

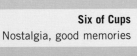

Seven of Cups
Wishful thinking, idealism

King of Cups
Unconditional love, a creative partner

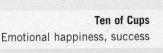
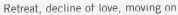

SWORDS

Ace of Swords
Innovation, prioritizing ideas

Eight of Swords
Blindness to the truth, lack of focus

Two of Swords
A balanced viewpoint

Nine of Swords
Being overwhelmed by negative thoughts

Three of Swords
Emotions blocking the truth

Ten of Swords
Mental back-stabbing

Four of Swords
Calmnes, reflection with objectivity

Page of Swords
An intelligent thinker, an enterprising man

Five of Swords
Defence of your viewpoint

Knight of Swords
Adventurous ideas, a romantic hero

Six of Swords
Progress, moving on to calmer times

Queen of Swords
Peacemaker, an intellectual woman

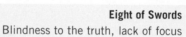

Seven of Swords
Unrealistic aims, too many ideas

King of Swords
Powerful mind, a judgemental man

CAV. DI BASTONI

CAVAL DI SPADI

PENTACLES

Ace of Pentacles
Abundance, contentment

Eight of Pentacles
Creative talent, working hard

Two of Pentacles
Juggling finances, changing situation

Nine of Pentacles
Realistic goals, material success

Three of Pentacle
Building resources, skilful action

Ten of Pentacles
Loving family, material wealth

Four of Pentacles
The power of possessions

Page of Pentacles
Belief in your talents, progress

Five of Pentacles
Feeling abandoned, material insecurity

Knight of Pentacles
Success, a prosperous lover

Six of Pentacles
Gifts, sharing out prosperity

Queen of Pentacles
Nurture, pleasure, a feminine soul

Seven of Pentacles
Harvest, re-evaluation of your skills

King of Pentacles
Business, attainment, an entrepreneur

The spreads

These are easy Tarot spreads to get you started – have a question or issue ready. The first four spreads give you answers to short-term issues, and use only Major Arcana cards; the last two are for longer-term issues. Incorporate Minor Arcana cards as soon as you feel confident.

Fortune spread

This spread can help you understand where you are now, what obstacles or influences are affecting you and where you are heading.

- Shuffle all the cards. Spread them out face-down on the table. Choose one card at a time while you concentrate on your issue or question.
- Lay your chosen cards out in the order shown below, face-up. Turn any reversed cards upright, facing you.

1 You now
2 Obstacles
3 Recent influences
4 Outcome

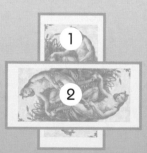

HOW TO INTERPRET THE SPREAD

- The first card represents 'you now', your current mood and the issues surrounding your question.
- The second card represents blockages or obstacles – whether psychological or literal – that concern you, whether or not you're aware of them.
- The third card refers to recent influences on you.
- The fourth card represents the outcome.
- As you look at the spread, check the keywords for each card and then the interpretations given in this book (see pages 17–31). Try to be objective. It often helps to compose a short story based around the cards.

EXAMPLE: **Should I end a love affair?**
1 You now – The Devil: This is a relationship based on sexual attraction.
2 Obstacles – The Sun: You're exaggerating the fun side and not looking at what else there is.
3 Recent Influences – The World: You've had a great time, but can it last for ever?
4 Outcome – The Moon: Rely on your gut feelings concerning what you want. Don't be blind to the truth, otherwise only more self-deception will follow.

'What do I need?' spread

This is a simple, yet revealing spread when you're not sure what you need in life or where you're going. Be honest with yourself and remember that your needs and wants will change over time.

- Shuffle all the cards as before, while concentrating on yourself.
- Lay the cards out in the order shown right, face-up.

1 Who am I? (now)
2 What/who do I need?
3 What/who *don't* I need?
4 Options available
5 Future direction

HOW TO INTERPRET THE SPREAD

- The first card represents you now.
- The second card is reflective of the positive things you need in your life: a specific type of partner, relationship, work, lifestyle and so on.
- The third card reflects the things that you *don't* need, which create conflict in your life, such as certain people, issues or work.
- The fourth card shows you how to deal with this and the various options available to you.
- The fifth card offers you direction on which decision to make, to put you on the right path.

EXAMPLE

1 Who am I? – The Tower: You're going through a period of disruption and your trust has been destroyed by unforeseen events.
2 What/who do I need? – The Emperor: A strong, active, independent partner, or self-sufficiency in your career.
3 What/who *don't* I need? – The Fool: Either a frivolous friend or lover, or taking risks.
4 Options available – Strength: Courage and honesty to ask for what you want or need.
5 Future direction – Wheel of Fortune: A chance encounter could change your life, so don't ignore what's on offer.

The mystic seven spread

Based on the shape of the Celtic cross, this spread adds a deeper analysis to any interpretation. Lay the cards out in the order shown right, face-up.

1 You now
2 Obstacles
3 Expectations
4 Past experiences relevant to the future
5 Recent influences
6 Immediate result
7 Outcome

HOW TO INTERPRET THE SPREAD

- The first card reveals what is going on in your life right now, your general mood and your issue or question.
- The second card represents the difficulties that confront you. This cross position holds the key to the whole spread, so try to interpret the first two cards together.

EXAMPLE: **I'm unsure of my current relationship and what is going to happen**

1 You now – Justice
2 Obstacles – Chariot: Everything seems to be going along easily (Justice), but your need to be in control (The Chariot) is upsetting the balance.

It could also be that frequent travel or a hectic lifestyle is making the relationship more unstable than you think.

- Next, interpret the two past cards, 4 and 5: the fourth card with regard to past experiences and the fifth to recent events that might need sorting out.
- Now interpret the two future cards, 3 and 6: your aspirations and secret longings, and imminent events or influences.
- Lastly, the outcome card, 7. A decision-making card, this defines direction in relation to your question and where it will lead you.

EXAMPLE

7 Outcome – Temperance: You must learn compromise and trust, and will have to moderate your personal desires if you are to succeed in your plans.

The relationship spread

This spread can help you understand a relationship at any point in time, identifying its plus and minus points and the key to its future.

- Shuffle all the cards as before, thinking clearly about your relationship before drawing them.
- Lay the cards out in the order shown right, face-up.

1 The relationship's energy
2 Its communication
3 Its strength
4 Its weakness
5 The reality
6 The passion
7 The key to the future

HOW TO INTERPRET THE SPREAD

- Each card represents the dynamic of the relationship. Remember that relationships are always developing, so be prepared for the dynamics to change too. This spread represents the 'engine-room' of the relationship and shows whether or not the components are in working order.

EXAMPLE: **I am involved with someone, but want to maintain my freedom – will the relationship work best like this?**

1 The relationship's energy – Temperance: Right now the energy is harmonious and balanced.

2 Its communication – The Star: You share similar ideals and can communicate openly.

3 Its strength – The Sun: The relationship's strength is its playful, light-hearted energy, so enjoy it for what it is.

4 Its weakness – The Chariot: You both have such busy, goal-oriented lives, which could put a strain on one or both of you.

5 The reality – The High Priestess: You're more emotionally involved than you admit.

6 The passion – The Hanged Man: Sexually, the relationship is in limbo, so where do you go from here? Can you sustain the passion?

7 The key to the future – The Lovers: Mutual honesty, freedom and making choices together will keep this relationship alive.

Horoscope spread

This is a very simple spread, based on the houses of the zodiac. It reveals the kind of experience you can expect in the next month in all areas of your life.

- Shuffle all the cards as before, thinking about the month ahead before drawing them.
- Lay the cards out in the order shown above, face-up.

1 Your personal quest
2 Money, values, possessions
3 Friends
4 Home
5 Romance, creativity, children
6 Rituals, body image, energy levels, health
7 Relationships, love
8 Sexuality
9 Travel
10 Career
11 Long-term goals
12 The past

HOW TO INTERPRET THE SPREAD

- Each card represents one different aspect of the month ahead.

EXAMPLE

1 Your personal quest – The Hermit: Discretion is called for, so reflect rather than be impulsive in your relationships.

2 Money, values, possessions – The Empress: Materially this is a good time for you and your finances will be more flexible.

3 Friends – Two of Swords: A friend will be difficult to get close to.

4 Home – Three of Pentacles: Time to get cracking on the DIY.

5 Romance, creativity, children – Ace of Pentacles: Romantic contentment.

6 Rituals, body image, energy levels, health – Temperance: Go on a diet.

7 Relationships, love – Ace of Swords: An innovative idea improves your flirtation skills.

8 Sexuality – King of Cups: You're sensitive to a lover's sexual needs.

9 Travel – The Hanged Man: You can't make up your mind where to hang out!

10 Career – Justice: Harmonious work contacts.

11 Long-term goals – The Star: You realize how to achieve a goal.

12 The past – Knight of Swords: A blast from the past sweeps into your life and out again.

The horseshoe spread

This spread adds an extra element to the future outcome cards, by using 'expected' and 'unexpected' placements. It was an old favourite with gypsy fortune-tellers.

• Shuffle all the cards as before, concentrating on your issue or question before drawing them.

• Lay the cards out in the order shown right, face-up.

1 Present situation
2 The expected
3 The unexpected
4 Immediate outcome
5 Long-term outcome

HOW TO INTERPRET THE SPREAD

• Each card represents a different aspect of your issue or question.

EXAMPLE: **I'm going through a career break – what shall I do next?**

1 Present situation – The Magician: Turn events in your favour, research and then decide what your true vocation is all about.

2 The expected – Six of Wands: You assume it's going to be a struggle doing something different, or that there will be confrontation with or resentment from friends or family.

3 The unexpected – Three of Cups: A surprise party, celebration or social event will change things for the better and give you the answer.

4 Immediate outcome – The Lovers: You begin to communicate with the right contacts and see where you're going next.

5 Long-term outcome – The Empress: Your decision to follow a creative profession will bring you great joy and success.

NUMEROLOGY

2 • NUMEROLOGY

Does one number seem to crop up in your life more than others? Perhaps you live at No. 3, your sister was born on the third day of the third month and you have three special friends. Numerology is the ancient art of divination based on the power of certain numbers.

What can numerology reveal about your future?

The alphabet provides a secret code for each of the single-digit numbers from 1 to 9, which have been used for thousands of years as a magical way to tell fortunes. According to Pythagoras – the father of numerology – numbers resonate to the powerful vibrations of the universe, particularly those between 1 and 9.

Numerology allows you to discover your unique combination of numbers, so that you can tap directly into the universal vibration and discover more about your secret desires, destiny and personality. You can also discover good dates for action; what kind of year you can expect and auspicious dates for making choices, when your personal number vibrates in harmony with the universal one. Numerology can also help you decide whether a new address, workplace or potential partner will be in harmony with your special numerical vibration.

The benefits of using numerology

- Determine your life path and follow your vocation.
- Find compatible companions, workplaces and addresses.
- Work out key dates for decision-making and specific actions.
- Reveal your secret desires.
- Change your name and destiny to suit you.
- Learn what challenges you need to overcome.

The history of numerology

Many ancient cultures believed in the significance and power of numbers, particularly the Greeks and Hebrews, who developed the systems used in modern-day numerology. It was the Greek mathematician and philosopher Pythagoras who wrote in the sixth century BCE, 'numbers are the first things of all of nature'. His theory was that everything was symbolized by, or reduced to, a number. Numbers were not just of mathematical significance, but were central to everything that went on in the universe: they were the key to all wisdom. The primary numbers, 1 to 9, each vibrate to a different frequency and these vibrations echo throughout the universe. This 'music of the spheres' was an expression of the heavenly bodies, which had their own numerical value and harmonic vibration.

Various symbols are used by different cultures to symbolize numbers, but the Pythagorean system, based on the nine primary numbers, is most common. By working out your 'birth-date' number and your 'name' number, you have immediate access to your life purpose and your talents, and to the most likely course that your future will take.

Left: Ancient Egyptian sacred numbers discovered at Karnak.

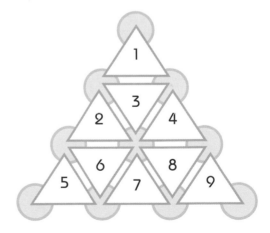

Above: Pythagorean number system pattern of ten pebbles.

The four main numbers in your life

There are four key numbers – personality, destiny, heart, expression – that determine the different aspects of your destiny and character.

Your personality number

This is worked out from your name. It describes your current character, the qualities you utilize in the world (both your strengths and weaknesses) and your skills. It reveals how you deal with change, make decisions and relate to others.

Your heart number

This number is made up of the numerical value of the vowels in your name. It reveals your secret desires, feelings, ideals and fantasies.

Your birth or destiny number

This number is worked out from your date of birth – a number you can't change, whether you like it or not! It refers to your life journey and the challenges, events and experiences you will encounter most frequently. It indicates your true vocation and your innate potential.

Your expression number

This is calculated from the numerical value of the consonants in your name. It reveals the image you show off or present to the world. This is not necessarily compatible with the secret you.

To find out your personality number

It's important to work with the name by which you are commonly known or the name by which you like to be known. For example, you might have been named Victoria Elizabeth Smith at birth, but prefer to be called Vicky Smith. You might have married, and are now known as Vicky Jones by all your friends and family, and like this name best. You might have changed your first name because you didn't like the one you were given. So which name do you feel most comfortable with? If you dislike your name and prefer being known by a nickname or a totally different name, use that instead.

An interesting exercise is to work out your personality number first from your given name at birth; then, if you've changed it in any way, work out the new number and see if they are different. Perhaps you've unconsciously changed your name to alter your life in some way, to adapt to people around you or to stand out from the crowd?

- Below is the Pythagorean alphabet code. All you have to do is look down the column to find which letter of your name corresponds to which number; add the numbers up, then reduce the final number to one digit between 1 and 9.
- For example, say your preferred name is Becky Green. B = 2, E = 5, C = 3, K = 2, Y = 7. So 2 + 5 + 3 + 2 + 7 = 19.
- G = 7, R = 9, E = 5, E= 5, N − 5. So 7 + 9 + 5 + 5 + 5 = 31.
- Add the first-name number to the last-name number: 1 + 9 + 3 + 1 = 14.
- Reduce this to one digit: 1+ 4 = 5.
- So the personality number for Becky Green is 5.

Pythagorean alphabet code

1	2	3	4	5	6	7	8	9
a	b	c	d	e	f	g	h	i
j	k	l	m	n	o	p	q	r
s	t	u	v	w	x	y	z	

Becky   Green
25327 = 19   79555 = 31
1+9+3+1 = 14
1+4 = 5

To find out your destiny number

Because this is calculated from your date of birth and cannot change, it reveals the life journey you will undertake. The more you fight the vibrational energy of this number in your life, the more challenges you will have to overcome. The best way to make your life what you want it to be is to express the associations of the number given through your lifestyle, work and relationships. Your destiny number is the easiest number to calculate.

- Add together all the numbers of your birth date. For example, say you were born on 16 June 1984. Write down the date in numerical form, then add the numbers up, like this:
  $1 + 6 + 6 + 1 + 9 + 8 + 4 = 35$.
- Reduce this down to one digit: $3 + 5 = 8$.
- Your destiny number is 8.

Date of birth

16 June 1984

$1 + 6 + 6 + 1 + 9 + 8 + 4 = 35$

$3 + 5 = 8$

Becky Green

$- 5 - - - \quad - - 55 -$

$5 + 5 + 5 = 15$

$1 + 5 = 6$ (heart number)

Becky Green

$2 - 327 \quad 79 - - 5$

$2 + 3 + 2 + 7 + 7 + 9 + 5 = 35$

$3 + 5 = 8$ (expression number)

6 (heart) $+ 8$ (expression) $= 14$

$1 + 4 = 5$ (personality number)

To find out your heart and expression numbers

- Write down the vowels from your name. In Becky Green's example, this would be: e, e, e.
- Write down the consonants for your name: here, b, c, k, y, g, r, n.
- To find the heart number, add up the numerical values of the vowels: $5 + 5 + 5 = 15$.
- Then reduce this to one digit: $1 + 5 = 6$.
- The heart number for Becky Green is therefore 6.
- To find the expression number, add up the numerical values of the consonants:
  $2 + 3 + 2 + 7 + 7 + 9 + 5 = 35$.
- Then reduce this to one digit: $3 + 5 = 8$.
- The expression number for Becky Green is therefore 8.
- Check that your adding up is correct by adding the heart number and the expression number together; this will give you the personality number.
  Here, 6 (heart number) + 8 (expression number) = 14, and $1 + 4 = 5$ (personality number).

Using numerology

If your personality and destiny numbers are both even or both odd, then they are said to be in harmony with each other. But if one is even and the other is odd, you may find that your life journey clashes with your personality and character.

Changing your name

If your personality number isn't compatible with your destiny number – one is even and one is odd – then it's possible to change your name, by adding another letter, dropping one or giving yourself a nickname, to give you the right number vibration. This means that the two compatible numbers will work in harmony and your life will run more smoothly. It's amazing how, if you change your name, you can alter your life for the better, just by the power of the numerical vibrations at work.

You can also check whether your potential married name is going to be compatible with your destiny number; and choose names for businesses, babies, pets and even best-selling books! First, though, become familiar with your own numbers and you will soon know which other numbers are going to work in harmony with yours.

Beckie   Greene
253295 = 26   795555 = 36
2+6+3+6 = 17
1+7 = 8

So that Becky's personality number is in harmony with her destiny number, Becky changed the spelling of her name to BECKIE GREENE.

2 + 5 + 3 + 2 + 9 + 5 = 26
7 + 9 + 5 + 5 + 5 + 5 = 36
2 + 6 + 3 + 6 = 17   1 + 7 = 8

Beckie's life should now run more smoothly as her personality number is in harmony with her destiny number 8.

TWO   Timing
256 = 13   294957 = 36
1+3 = 4   3+6 = 9
9+4 = 13
1+3 = 4

- Beckie Greene wrote a romantic novel. To ensure it's success she called the book 'Two Timing'.
  2 + 5 + 6 = 13
  1 + 3 = 4
  2 + 9 + 4 + 9 + 5 + 7 = 36
  3 + 6 = 9
  9 + 4 = 13   1 + 3 = 4

4 is a number of success and also compatible with her destiny number.

Choosing a secret name

Your birth name is important – it's official, but then again it was 'given' to you. A choice was probably made about your identity before you were even born. Your given name is in fact your parents' projection (usually unconscious) of who they want you to be. And that name is also a number they have coincidentally chosen for you. Even though you might have changed your name to a nickname or a totally different name, having a secret name that no one (except you) knows can empower you with qualities for which you perhaps secretly long, or believe are lacking in your life.

A secret name can make you happier, wiser, richer, funnier, more assertive and compassionate; it can boost your ego or give you a good self-image to bring you fortune or luck.

- Choose a number that seems to correspond to the qualities you are looking for or feel that you lack. Then choose a name that has the right number total. It could be anything from Jack to Aphrodite, but it must also be a name you like.
- For example, Beckie Green wants to be more extrovert so she choses number 1. Her secret name when reduced down to one digit is 1.
- Write down your chosen name on a piece of paper nine times, then burn the paper or bury it in a secret place.

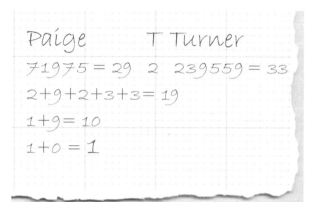

- Repeat your secret name to yourself nine times before you go to sleep and nine times when you wake up.
- Repeat your secret name over and over again, like a mantra, whenever you feel the need to boost your ego, or invoke those qualities associated with the number. Say your mantric name in your head when meeting new people or encountering situations in which you feel insecure or confused. If you feel that you don't need your secret name any more, or require a different one, you can change it at any time.

9 October 2006

$9 + 1 + 0 + 2 + 0 + 0 + 6 = 18$

$1 + 8 = 9$

$9 \text{ (date)} + 8 \text{ (destiny)} = 17$

$1 + 7 = 8$

Choosing a special date

Numerology is great for planning ahead, for choosing auspicious dates for any occasion, whether it's a wedding, a visit to the bank manager or even finding a new lover. Say, for example, that you want to set up a business on an auspicious day, and you think 8 October 2006 is a good date:

$8 + 1 + 0 + 2 + 0 + 0 + 6 = 17.$

$1 + 7 = 8.$

The number 8 is very powerful, considered extremely lucky in China and symbolizes material wealth and success. This is a truly auspicious date for setting up a business. But you must now add it to your *own* destiny number, to see whether for you personally it will be fortunate or not. Let's take Becky Green again, whose destiny number is also 8. This means that success and status are very important to her and although the date is the same as her destiny number, see what happens when they merge:

$8 + 8 = 16, 1 + 6 = 7.$

The number 7 is the number of escapism and dreaminess, and hardly gels with 8, which is about the world of achievement. I would suggest that for Becky Green, 8 October 2006 is not a good date. Instead, I would suggest 9 October, because, if added to her destiny number, this would result in the desired number: 8.

Finding out about the year ahead

You can check out your personal year ahead, evaluating the kind of energy, events and trends that will arise and preparing yourself to make any necessary changes accordingly.

- First, calculate your personal year number, by adding up the numbers of the year in question and reducing them to a single digit. For example, for 2007: $2 + 7 = 9$.
- Next, add just the day and month of your birth, leaving out your year. Becky Green's date of birth was 16 June, so $1 + 6 + 6 = 13; 1 + 3 = 4$.
- Now add the year number to the month and day number, so: $9 + 4 = 13; 1 + 3 = 4$.
- 2007 is therefore going to be a No. 4 year for Becky, which is the year of family values, structure and hard work. But she must try not to get bogged down in routines.

2007: $2 + 0 + 0 + 7 = 9$

16 June: $1 + 6 + 6 = 13$

$1 + 3 = 4$

$9 + 4 = 13$

$1 + 3 = 4$

Compatibility grid

You can also use numerology to see how compatible you are with someone else – whether it's a potential lover, friend or boss. Work out their personality number as for your own, then check the grid below to see how you match up.

One/one	Competitive, exciting
One/two	Sensual, indulgent
One/three	Mischievous, fun
One/four	Confusing, dramatic
One/five	Dynamic, creative
One/six	Defensive, moody
One/seven	Unreliable, escapist
One/eight	Driven, controlling
One/nine	Motivated, spirited
Two/two	Friendly, serene
Two/three	Unpredictable, sexy
Two/four	Warm, materialistic
Two/five	Original, focused
Two/six	Ambitious, settled
Two/seven	Erratic, defensive
Two/eight	Organized, successful
Two/nine	Challenging, steamy
Three/three	Hilarious, light-hearted
Three/four	Happy, sizzling
Three/five	Heavenly, wicked
Three/six	Sensible, progressive
Three/seven	Dreamy, romantic
Three/eight	Passionate, driven
Three/nine	Restless, adventurous
Four/four	Easy, calm
Four/five	Rousing, tenacious
Four/six	Determined, reassuring
Four/seven	Suspicious, fragmented
Four/eight	Successful, complete
Four/nine	Impressive, sexy
Five/five	Idyllic, madcap
Five/six	Obscure, divided
Five/seven	Enchanting, ethereal
Five/eight	Carnal, luxurious
Five/nine	Extravagant, imaginative
Six/six	Faultless, idealistic
Six/seven	Peaceful, laid-back
Six/eight	Physical, worldly
Six/nine	Compassionate, easy-going
Seven/seven	Emotional, soppy
Seven/eight	Provocative, edgy
Seven/nine	Communicative, creative
Eight/eight	Sensitive, intense
Eight/nine	Unpredictable, volatile
Nine/nine	Mercurial, wild

The meaning of the numbers

Each number has a separate interpretation for its destiny, personality, heart and expression categories. Your personality number may be very different to your destiny number, and so on. Read each meaning carefully and relate it to your current wishes, desires and feelings.

One

The sun, yellow, wholeness, unity

Keywords Single-mindedness, independence

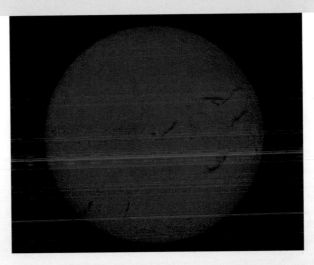

The sun traditionally symbolizes potential and oneness.

DESTINY NUMBER

You were born to be a leader and your life journey will be filled with competitive rivals because you will make an impact wherever you go. Pioneering and spirited, you won't let anyone stop you from aiming high and your original ideas are often ahead of the times. Your ambitions need expression and realization.

Try to avoid Putting other people second, feeling superior, taking risks.

Future potential Be number one and embrace a free, creative lifestyle that will bring the changes you seek. Choose a vocation where you are the boss.

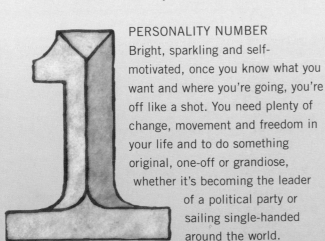

PERSONALITY NUMBER

Bright, sparkling and self-motivated, once you know what you want and where you're going, you're off like a shot. You need plenty of change, movement and freedom in your life and to do something original, one-off or grandiose, whether it's becoming the leader of a political party or sailing single-handed around the world.

Relationship You find it hard to let anyone get really close to you, but are a spontaneous lover and a hilarious and warm friend.

HEART NUMBER

Secretly, you want to be an innovator. You know that you could be a leader, and independence is vital to your well-being. You feel passionately, and would love to be a film star or celebrity.

EXPRESSION NUMBER

You're so confident in social circles that people sometimes think you're arrogant. You make friends easily and are usually surrounded by an entourage of admirers of the opposite sex. On the surface you appear to know what you're doing, but often it's a big bluff for deeper insecurities.

Two

The moon, rhythm, dance, yin and yang, moonstone

Keywords Negotiation, partnership

DESTINY NUMBER

You are a born negotiator. Cooperative and adaptable, you know how to keep everyone happy. You'd rather work behind the scenes and let others make all the decisions. You don't like arguments and often give in too easily to other people's demands for the sake of peace. Your life journey will be coloured by many different, enticing relationships.

Try to avoid Resenting others because you didn't stand up for yourself; always making compromises.

Future potential Utilize your diplomatic skills. Choose a vocation where you can be a great mediator.

PERSONALITY NUMBER

Everyone loves having you around, because you're so eager to make them feel good about themselves. But you can be a little clingy about your friends, your family, your job or the past. Emotionally sensitive, you can soothe any furrowed brow.

Relationship You're incredibly protective, but can retreat into your shell when you feel threatened. You need someone who is sensitive and creative like you.

HEART NUMBER

Deep down you're very sensitive and need total emotional closeness to feel comfortable in a relationship. Secretly, you desire lots of money, possessions and a family to belong to. Start saving, working hard and feel enriched by the clan of people around you.

EXPRESSION NUMBER

You just can't help but relate to others on a one-to-one basis. People see you as diplomatic and fair, gentle and sensitive. Your tact and discretion mean that others confide in you. But do you like carrying everyone else's troubles for them? This could be difficult, if your personality or destiny number is more self-centred.

Yin is passive, yang is active; together they create harmony.

Three

Jupiter, spring, growth, amethyst

Keywords Creativity, communication

DESTINY NUMBER

You're a born communicator, and need to express yourself through a creative outlet. Your life journey will consist of many love relationships, much travel and light-hearted living. You have a natural gift for words and a great sense of adventure. If you're not being challenged, you will find something to fight against. You're an active agent in life and won't let opportunities pass you by.

Try to avoid Trusting everyone you meet.

Future potential Choose a busy vocation in the media or the arts. Expand your horizons and enjoy being the flirtatious, fun-loving person you were destined to be.

Number Three people are like spring blossom bursting into life.

PERSONALITY NUMBER

Extrovert and entertaining, you love the company of others and believe that life's for living to the full. You get restless if your work or relationships are monotonous or dull. And you prefer the unpredictable and exciting to the tried and trusted. Success matters to you and you always look to the future rather than dwell on the past.

Relationship Flirtatious and seductive, you're not the most constant of companions, but you always adore the one you're with and take each day as it comes.

HEART NUMBER

Deep down you're a secret romantic. You wish you could travel the world in search of the perfect partner, even if you're already settled. Your innermost desire is to write a best-selling novel or film script, or even to become a philosopher. None of these is out of reach.

EXPRESSION NUMBER

Everyone thinks you're confident, generous and fun to have around. You adore all the attention and love the challenge of new ideas and self-opinionated people. You communicate easily and have a busy social life. Your expression number will get you places – so don't be afraid to use it.

Four

Saturn, the four seasons, dark green, structure

Keywords Stability, will power

DESTINY NUMBER

You're a born organizer. Practical and self-willed, you have the motivation to achieve whatever you set out to do. Ambitious, capable and trustworthy, your life journey will consist of enterprising work and events that will force you to become self-sufficient and successful.

Try to avoid Being too rigid in your views. Don't get bogged down in routine.

Future potential Utilize your natural organizational skills. Success is assured if you take things one step at a time and take time out to play a little, too.

PERSONALITY NUMBER

Being practical and down-to-earth, friends know they can depend on you in a crisis. You love making plans for the future, and then following them through. You enjoy the great outdoors and have an affinity with animals and nature. Nurture your ability to build solid structures and create financial security.

Relationship You're loyal and constant, and need to be the power behind your partner's throne as well as your own.

HEART NUMBER

You secretly hate change and like to be in control of your life. Acutely vulnerable, you compensate by being the epitome of efficiency and common sense. Your secret desire is to be head of the company – or perhaps even an industrial spy. Why not?

EXPRESSION NUMBER

You are reliable, stable and trustworthy. Often perceived as a bit of a workaholic, you have incredible stamina and get things done without fuss. Utilize this gift of self-discipline, for it will bring you much happiness, whatever destiny number you are.

The planet Saturn symbolizes stability, security and self-control.

Five

Mercury, yellow, creativity, pentacles

Keywords Adventure, travel

DESTINY NUMBER

You're a born traveller, ready to try anything once. Your life journey will be filled with fascinating encounters and your restless sense of adventure will lead you down many different roads. You have excellent communicative skills, wit, charm and an eagerness for knowledge and experience. Your versatility can be put to great use in working with the public.
Try to avoid Getting restless and bored.
Future potential Widen your horizons, live abroad, work in a vocation that gets you travelling, and unleash your wild side.

Exotic locations empower Number Five people with vitality.

PERSONALITY NUMBER

Impulsive and freedom-loving, you hate being tied down, and can't bear life to be dull or routine. If you're not on your travels, you will seek out adventurous experiences for the sake of change. You always look ahead and never back. Enthusiastic about your next job, next quest, next lover – you name it, there's always something new and fascinating to be explored in life.
Relationship Free-spirited and romantic, you need someone who respects your independence and gives you bags of space.

HEART NUMBER

Deep down you're restless. You want a more exciting lifestyle, but fear what others will think if you rebel against their standards. Your secret desire is to live a nomadic life. Perhaps it's time to follow your dream?

EXPRESSION NUMBER

You're great company and friends can't get enough of your live-wire attitude to life. Gossipy and mentally sharp, you like to prove you know a lot about everything. You express your ideas well, but cover up your feelings. The adaptable side of your nature means that you can make changes to suit you.

Six

Venus, harmony, luxury, turquoise

Keywords Compassion, idealism

DESTINY NUMBER

You're a born protector of others. Being altruistic and kind, your friends, family and partner come first. Your life journey will be about nurturing others and making them feel good about themselves. You need routine, rituals and family values to make you feel secure. Express your generosity and understanding of human nature through the healing arts.

Try to avoid Being too noble and selfless, for it can make you resentful rather than helpful.

Future potential It's essential that you work as part of a team, or be of service in some way, to bring out your nurturing side. But don't let others decide your future for you.

PERSONALITY NUMBER

Family and domestic harmony are most important to you and you're willing to help everyone achieve their goals. A bit of a matchmaker, you involve yourself in other people's personal problems and then become over-protective. You're great with money and have very high standards at work and at home.

Relationship You need a warm, loving relationship and a secure home life. You thrive with a partner who is luxury-loving and loyal.

HEART NUMBER

Your domestic and family life are much more important to you than others think, and you want to be loved with as much warmth as you give out. Your secret desire is to have a luxurious lifestyle, surrounded by a huge family or a million friends. Go for it!

EXPRESSION NUMBER

On the surface you're great company and your easy-going attitude makes people feel immediately at ease. Understanding what makes people tick can put you ahead of any professional competition and your charm will win you many brownie points.

Carry a piece of turquoise with you for good luck.

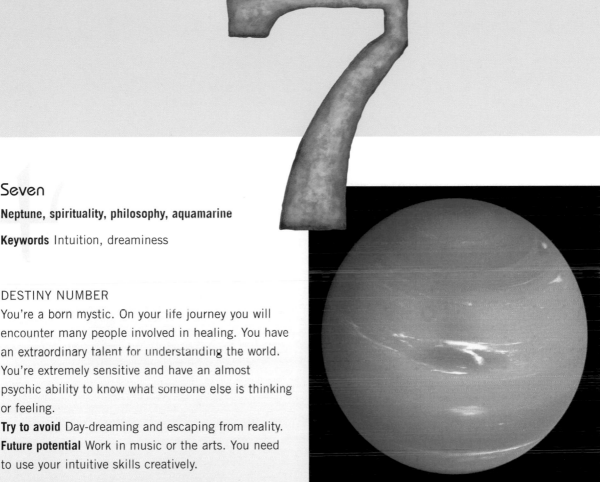

Seven

Neptune, spirituality, philosophy, aquamarine

Keywords Intuition, dreaminess

DESTINY NUMBER

You're a born mystic. On your life journey you will encounter many people involved in healing. You have an extraordinary talent for understanding the world. You're extremely sensitive and have an almost psychic ability to know what someone else is thinking or feeling.

Try to avoid Day-dreaming and escaping from reality.

Future potential Work in music or the arts. You need to use your intuitive skills creatively.

Number Seven people are in touch with mystical Neptune.

PERSONALITY NUMBER

You like to be on your own sometimes and your secretive side means that others find it difficult to get close to you. You are almost psychic in your ability to suss people out. Gentle, serene and a dreamer, you seem to operate in a totally different way from everyone else.

Relationship You need a partner who won't mind you drifting off into space.

HEART NUMBER

Deep down you know that the world isn't quite what it seems. You have odd moments of psychic connection to people. Music, art and the occult mean more to you than is apparent on the surface. Your secret desire is to be a mystic, spiritual guru or white witch. Liberate your healing power.

EXPRESSION NUMBER

On the surface you seem moody, dreamy and in a world of your own. Other people find it difficult to work you out, and you take ages before you let anyone get close to you. You sometimes forget what you're saying in the middle of a sentence, and at other times have extraordinary knowledge to divulge.

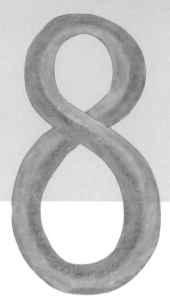

Eight

Capricorn, winter, destiny, materialism

Keywords Ambition, proficiency

DESTINY NUMBER

You're a born entrepreneur. The most important thing in your life will be status, prestige and success. The drive to achieve at all costs means that you put relationships second. Your life journey will be one of sheer hard work and material ambitions. Your power-seeking efficiency will lead you to the top of your profession.

Try to avoid Assuming everyone has the same motivation or goals as you.

Future potential Aim for perfect results, prove your worth and focus on material achievement.

Number Eight people are as cool as winter, but sure of their direction.

PERSONALITY NUMBER

You feel driven to get on in life, and often prefer working day and night to forming relationships. Incredibly self-sufficient, you go to extraordinary lengths to stay in control of your personal world, but can become too authoritarian towards others. Your dogmatic attitude brings you results, but you find it difficult to relax.

Relationship You prefer working relationships to loving ones. But if you can combine the two, you will create an enterprising partnership.

HEART NUMBER

You have a secret inner drive for success and power, and you feel cheated if you don't achieve material results. Deep down you're organized and dependable, however scatty you appear on the surface. Your secret desire is to be richer than Richard Branson and Bill Gates, or to run the world.

EXPRESSION NUMBER

Organized, efficient and highly dependable, you're not afraid of hard work and are always well dressed, stylish and money-conscious. You can appear to be bossy and self-righteous, and your thirst for worldly achievement means that you don't have many allies. Only a few, select friends are allowed into your private world.

Nine

Mars, the universe, red, idealist, visionary

Keywords Competitiveness, outspokenness

DESTINY NUMBER

You're a born campaigner for everyone else's causes and have great enthusiasm for new enterprises. Throughout your life journey you will be challenged by injustices and will fight for the freedom of others, whether on a global or personal scale. You have extraordinary visions for the future, but you don't always follow things through.

Try to avoid Making promises and then ducking out at the last minute.

Future potential You will have many career changes in your life. Be prepared to adapt and you will soon find the happiness you're hoping for.

PERSONALITY NUMBER

Romantic, selfless and free-spirited, you're often the centre of attention. You adore roaming around the world, meeting strangers and rushing off impulsively to do or see something different or new. Humanitarian and honest, you will help the underdog first. You love the intrigue of clandestine love affairs and the power of knowing other people's secrets.

Nines are often great campaigners against injustice and can also be as flashy as a vibrant poppy.

Relationship You find it hard to stay in a long-term commitment unless your partner is as free-spirited as you. Romance and intrigue are more important to you than home comforts and routine love.

HEART NUMBER

Deep down you're a closet romantic, who wants to be led astray or seduce your way through life. Your secret desire is to travel the world or be a free spirit. Unleash that wild side and enjoy!

EXPRESSION NUMBER

On the surface you're charm personified. Your enthusiasm for life is very infectious and people just love having you around. But when relationships start to get too intense or serious, you disappear or find new social contacts. You hate being pinned down. Yet if someone asks you for help or advice, you're the first to be at their door.

PALMISTRY

3 • PALMISTRY

Palmistry is the ancient art of reading character and destiny from your palm. There are three distinct areas of study: dermatoglyphics (skin patterns), chirognomy (shape) and chiromancy (lines and marks). Here you will learn how to combine chiromancy and chirognomy.

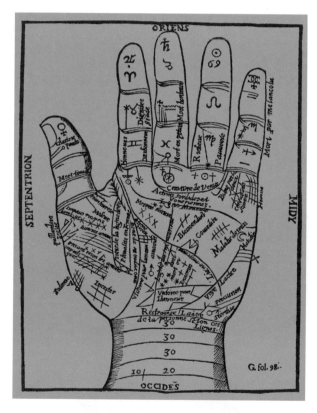

A 17th-century woodcut of all the major lines and mounts of the left hand.

What can palmistry reveal about your future?

Your palm holds the key not only to your unique personality, it also represents the kind of life journey you will have – like a map that reveals who you are and where you're going. The pattern of lines on your hand is unique to you. By knowing more about your personal goals and character, you will be able to take control of your destiny, rather than feeling that life is fated or that you have no choices. By learning about the meanings behind the shape, lines, mounts and fingers of your major hand (the hand you write with), you can see where you are going in life and what kind of relationships and career are right for you. Read your palm and you read into the future, because with knowledge of your character and calling you can take charge of your destiny.

The benefits of using palmistry

- Find the kind of love that suits you as an individual.
- Gain direction and goals to aim for.
- Make life-changing decisions.
- Understand your hidden potential.
- Know your true vocation.
- Determine your life path.

A highly decorative painted manuscript reveals the secrets of Holy Mother Anne's palm. She was revered in the 18th century.

The history of palmistry

Ancient cultures, such as those of India, Egypt and China, practised palmistry as long ago as 5,000 years. Some sources believe that Western palmistry is based on physiognomy – the art of understanding someone's personality and future by their facial features – and that it dates back to 1100 BCE.

Palmistry was used by the ancient Greeks, such as Hippocrates and Galen, as an aid in medicine, and around 3000 BCE the Emperor of China used his thumbprint to seal documents. The earliest written manuscript that documents palmistry in the English language is dated 1440 and is known as the Digby Roll IV.

Palmistry was thought to be a kind of devil-worship by the early Christian Church and was subsequently outlawed. But gypsies, Romanies and many mystics carried on practising the art in secret right up until the end of the 19th century. Popularized by psychic performers such as Cheiro, an Irish fortune-teller whose real name was Count Louis Harmon, palmistry became the most popular of all the divinatory arts in the first part of the 20th century, but was thereafter treated as a parlour game. It is now becoming increasingly popular once again, not only for telling your fortune, but also for guidance on self-development and understanding.

Hand shapes

There are four basic hand shapes closely connected to the four elements: earth, fire, air and water. Your hand gives an immediate indication of your basic personality, and knowing more about who you are means that you can work on your skills and talents to shape your future.

Identifying your hand shape

Discover the overall shape of your major hand (the one you write with) by holding it up in front of you with the palm facing you. Then look at the illustrations to determine which shape is closest to yours.

Earth element:

SQUARE OR 'PRACTICAL' HAND
Hand type Square palm with short fingers
Keywords Common sense, practical ability
You are honest, physically strong and have a very down-to-earth approach to life. You view life with a realistic, humorous approach, and can do well in any of the practical or creative arts. Patient and very fixed in your ways, you are loving and loyal. But you also need to be needed. Teamwork, a good social life and plenty of challenges keep you content and motivated.
Future potential Keep physically busy, express your practical skills and your love of beauty. Give yourself deadlines and get to know people who are sensitive to your needs, and your dreams will come true.

Fire

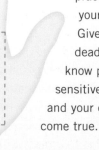

Earth

Fire element:

ENERGETIC OR 'INTUITIVE' HAND
Hand type A long palm with medium-length fingers
Keywords Restlessness, animation
You just want to get on with life. Passionate and restless, you need lots of physical exercise and mental stimulation. Your fiery attitude to others can get you into confrontations, but you thrive on challenge and adventure. You hate wasting time and get things done as quickly as possible, without worrying about the consequences. Other people envy your self-motivation.
Future potential Get involved in relationships that give you room to breathe, and a career that will be fast-paced and challenging. You need to lead in order to succeed.

Air element:

INTELLECTUAL OR 'BALANCED' HAND

Hand type A square palm with long fingers

Keywords Cleverness, idealism

Communication and knowledge keep you alert and inspired. You have a brilliant mind and, with a logical, objective approach to life, you are more able to cope with the highs and lows than others. You're suited to work where you can transmit or research information. Idealistic in love relationships, you believe utterly in romance.

Future potential Involve yourself in the world of communication or the media, making sure that you learn something new every day.

Water

Water element:

SENSITIVE OR POINTED HAND

Hand type Slim palm, long fingers

Keywords Emotions, artistic ability

Extremely sensitive to your surroundings, you are psychic and intuitive. You're a true romantic, and often get involved in clandestine love affairs. Because you are dreamy and unrealistic, real life seems harsh, so you escape into your imagination rather than face the truth. Gregarious one day and private the next, you are always generous with your time.

Future potential Unleash your musical or artistic talents and be rewarded. Develop your self-esteem and your love life will change for the better.

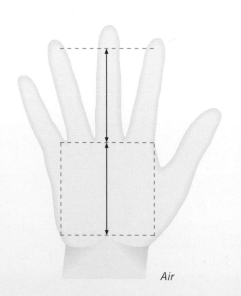

Air

Fingers and thumbs

The shapes of your fingers and thumbs reveal more about your personality and potential. When assessing them, look at the overall shape and ignore the nails. Look for the shape that repeats most frequently, as your digits might be a mixture of long, short, square and so on.

The thumb

This represents the amount of energy you exude and whether you're a leader or a follower. The larger the thumb in comparison with your hand, the stronger your personality.

Small or short thumb

Full of passive energy, you can be very sensitive. Work in a peaceful environment where you don't have to make key decisions.

Long thumb

You're determined to succeed and need to be in a position to make decisions.

Pointed thumb

You have creative talent, but are an idealist, so work with a team.

Square-tipped thumb

Practical and efficient, you need to lead from the top.

Bulbous thumb

You're temperamental, but you get things done. You're better working alone.

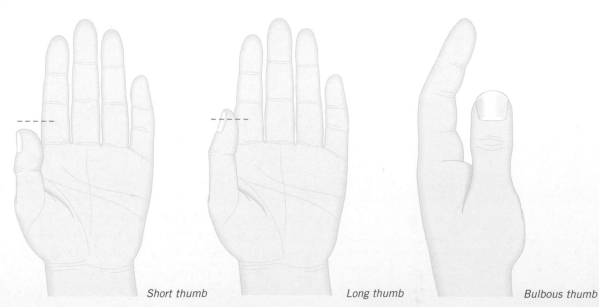

Short thumb　　　　*Long thumb*　　　　*Bulbous thumb*

The fingers

There are four basic types of finger shape and, depending on the average shape of your fingertips, you can determine which lifestyle suits you best.

Conical fingertips

Instinctively you know how to act in any situation. You're wise, non-judgemental and always willing to give other people advice or help. You can work out what people are thinking and feeling, and you'd do well with a career in the healing professions.

Pointed fingertips

You work best in a beautiful or aesthetically pleasing environment. Good taste matters to you and you have an eye for detail, design and colour. You can be fussy about what you wear and how you look, but your stylish charisma gets you noticed. You thrive in an orderly environment.

Square fingertips

You're motivated and down-to-earth, but you prefer a simple, laid-back lifestyle where you've got time to enjoy other pleasures. Professional and successful, you can make money easily in business ventures and property deals. You prefer working in a conventional environment and don't like rebellious colleagues or too much change.

Spatulate (spreading) fingertips

Mentally and physically active, you adapt well to travel, adventure, the great outdoors and a busy lifestyle. Working 24/7 doesn't faze you, but you need time out to enjoy good social interaction, too. You're highly intelligent and thrive in a lively, light-hearted environment with like-minded people.

The mounts

Mounts are the soft, spongy pads under the base of each finger (also found in other areas of the palm). They are not all developed in everyone, but any mounts that you have will give you further clues to your personality, reinforcing other strong characteristics.

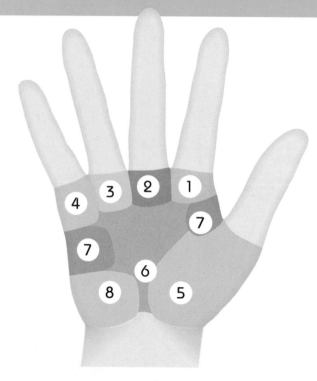

The eight main mounts

1 Jupiter mount
Found under the first finger. If it's well developed, it reveals that you're confident and ambitious.

2 Saturn mount
A mount under the middle finger. When well developed, it indicates that you have a very balanced mind.

3 Apollo mount
Located at the base of the third finger. When well developed, this mount reveals that you're understanding and creative.

4 Mercury mount
Found under the third and little finger. If it's well developed, you are a good business communicator. If the mount is flat, you need to develop your communication skills.

5 Venus mount
The fleshy area at the base of thumb. If it's well rounded, you enjoy the simple pleasures of life, family is important to you and you are warm-hearted.

6 Neptune mount
Found at the middle base of the palm. When well developed, it indicates that you are very sensitive towards other people's needs.

7 Mars mounts
Two adjacent mounts at the centre of the palm, just below the digital mounts. If this area is well developed, you have bags of energy, but are often impulsive and impetuous.

8 Lunar mount
The area halfway down the outer edge of the palm towards the wrist. If this is firm, it signifies compassion, sensitivity and creativity. If it's more prominent than the other mounts on your palm, you are easily influenced by others and don't trust your own instincts.

The major lines

There are four main lines on the hands, as summarized below. They are described in greater detail on pages 68–75.

Interpreting the lines on your palm

1 Life line

This line describes your vitality, the potential of your life journey, your family connections and your lifestyle.

2 Heart line

As the name suggests, this line reveals all matters relating to love, romance, happiness and your emotional life.

3 Head line

This describes your mental outlook on life, possible career directions and creative abilities.

4 Fate line

The fate line reveals your motivation, your career direction and how much in control of your life you are.

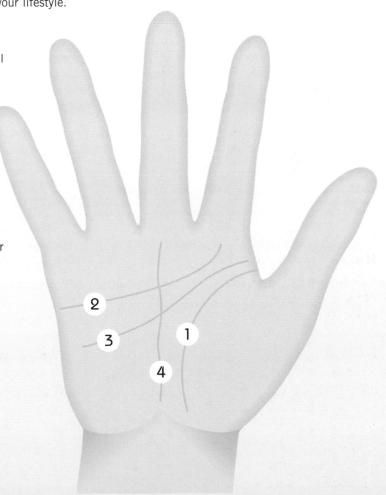

The life line

This line starts above the thumb and curves down towards the wrist. There are many variations.

1 Life line curves widely towards middle of hand

You want to achieve great things in your life. Travel, adventure and the unknown will lure you on. Independence matters to you and you want to prove that you're different from everyone else, with ground-breaking ideas.

2 Life line stays near thumb

Home is where you feel most content. You're not particularly ambitious, but you do yearn for a good family life and to feel wanted and special.

3 Life line ends by veering towards outer side of wrist

This often reveals that you will emigrate or move a long way from home. Your best experiences will come from travelling or living overseas.

4 Life line starts from base of index finger

You need a constant change of lifestyle to keep you content. You're strong-willed and determined to do your own thing your way.

5 Life line appears to cut down through the mount of Venus

You are living a very restricted life, perhaps under the influence of family members or society's expectations. Change this by realizing that approval and love are not the same thing. Be loved for who you are, not for what others think you should be.

6 Breaks in the life line

These simply signify many changes in your life, as one cycle ends and another begins. A lot of overlapping breaks in the line indicate that the transformation is positive and that you will be the one making the choice.

7 Double life line

There are two possibilities:
a) You may have a twin or a guardian angel.
b) You lead a double life. For example, you live in two different countries; have two lovers; work in high finance by day, while by night you gamble!

8 Life line branches towards wrist

This indicates much travel, and the wider or longer the fork, the more important journeys will be in your life, perhaps colouring your whole lifestyle package.

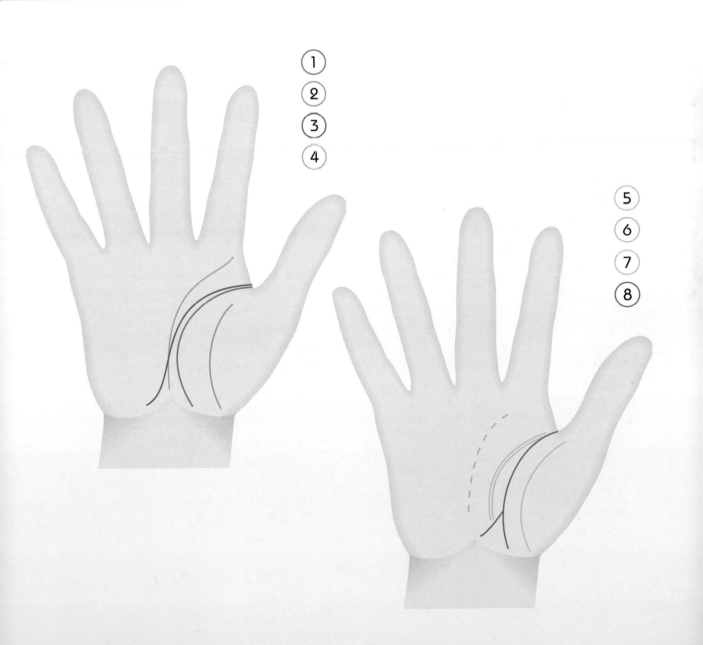

The heart line

The heart line starts at the outer edge of your hand beneath your little finger and curves or aims straight across the palm.

1 Heart line is strong, well defined or dominant

You will find that love affairs, romance and relationships will be key themes and signposts in your life journey.

2 Heart line is very short, thin or weak

This can indicate that you aren't in touch with your own feelings. You may be a bit of an approval seeker and sex may be more important to you in a relationship than emotional involvement.

3 Heart line starts high up, close to base of little finger across top of hand

You are very self-conscious and put up major emotional defences. You can be highly self-critical, more interested in the intellectual or mental side of a relationship than in emotional commitment.

4 Heart line starts low, beneath the outside knuckle of the palm

Idealistic and romantic, you are in love with love itself and expect too much from your partners. You often feel let down when the romance has faded and can flit from affair to affair in the hope that someone will live up to your image of perfection.

5 Heart line ends between first finger and middle two fingers

Emotional, passionate and seductive, you make it clear who's in charge of the relationship. It's all or nothing when you fall for someone and you will move mountains to be with the one you love.
You exude charisma and will have many admirers, lovers or partners along the way.

6 Heart line ends beneath middle finger

You like to be in charge of any relationship, and family, structure and conventional expectations matter to you. Long-term love is more important than one-off affairs and you're good at building a successful working relationship.

7 Heart line ends beneath first finger

You're open and free-spirited in love and will have very successful relationships, as long as you maintain your freedom. You are a friend as well as a lover, adaptable and easy-going.

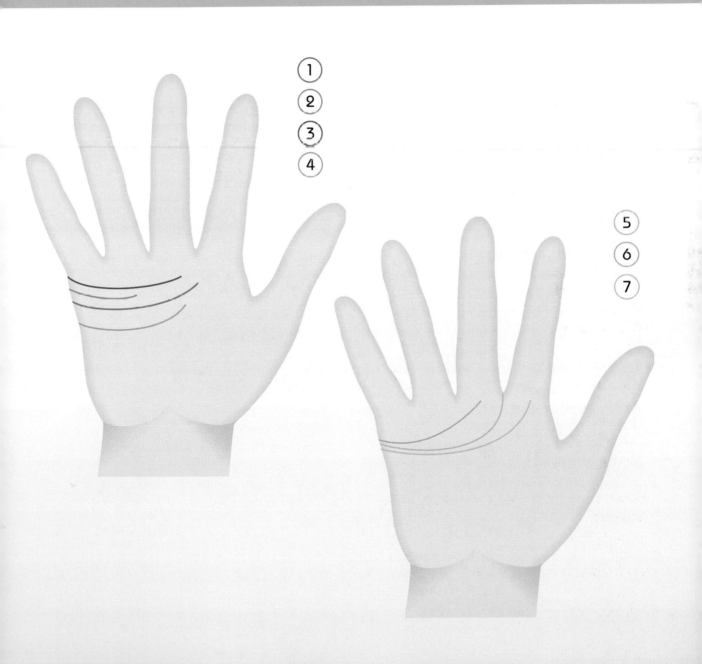

The head line

This line is usually found between the heart and life lines. It starts between the thumb and first finger and runs across the centre of the palm, ending towards the outer side of your hand. If the line is strong and wide, you're methodical and willing to get a job done; if thin, faint or short, you find it difficult to make decisions or order your mind. A very long head line indicates that you get lost in thought, but are able to see both sides of an argument.

1 Head line and life line joined together at the start

Early on in life you find it difficult to separate from your family or upbringing. You have little self-confidence and worry about what others think about you. Luckily, you will compensate for this later on by establishing your own independence and ambitions.

2 Head line not joined to life line

Free-thinking, self-willed and enthusiastic about everything you do, you will get on in life without worrying about what other people think. You are very focused and rely only on yourself.

3 Head line rises under index finger

Ambitious and motivated, you are competitive and convinced that you can beat any opposition. Your larger-than-life approach gets you places, but you sometimes believe you can get away with anything.

4 Head line travels straight across palm, from inner to outer edge

Always focused and in control of your life, you need material security. Generous with your time and money, you can be self-obsessed with clothes, possessions and the way you look.

5 Head line dips downwards

Sensitive and moody, you are also extremely intuitive and imaginative. You're artistic, creative and like to be on your own a lot. You work well in an artistic, laid-back environment free from stress.

6 Head line ends in a fork

If the line splits into two at the end, it's a sign of a born writer or communication talent. If the fork is very pronounced, you will successfully work in journalism or the media.

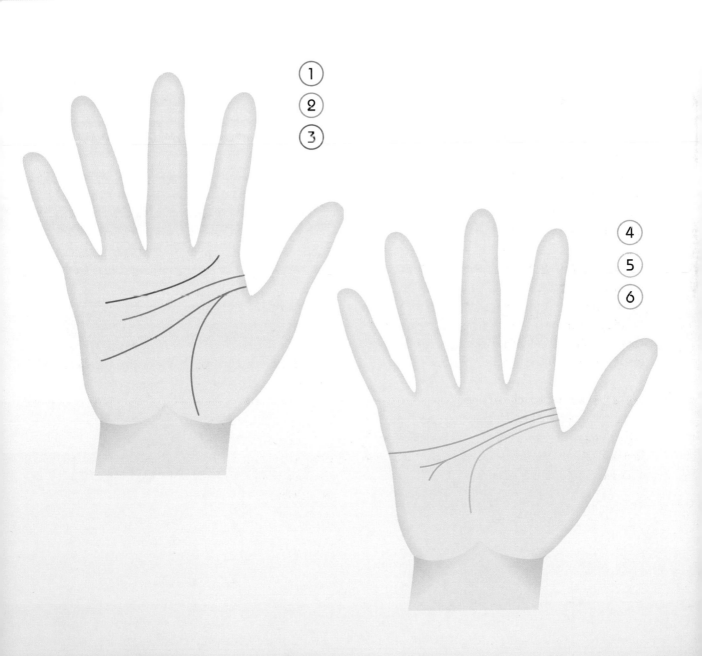

The fate line

Concerning career, work and ambition, the fate line starts from a point at the bottom of the palm, running up to the top, near the base of the fingers.

1 Fate line runs up middle of palm and ends beneath middle finger

You know what you want and where you're going. If you dedicate yourself to your ambitions, you will achieve much success and good fortune.

2 Fate line starts on the outer palm opposite the thumb

Independent and hot-headed, you are keen to break away from family or traditional expectations. You need to travel or live abroad, widen your perspective on life and you will find true success and achievement.

3 Fate line veers towards first finger

Dedicated to your career or profession, you will achieve what you set out to do. You will stand out from the crowd and receive much acclaim. This is often the sign of a true leader.

4 Fate line short or faint

You aren't particularly ambitious and often feel other people are too obsessed with success and achievement. You work well in a laid-back, low-pressure environment with lots of friends.

5 Breaks in the fate line

You will have many changes of direction in your career and life. You never really dedicate yourself to one thing, so be prepared for success to come and go. However, you have an extraordinary talent for adapting to each new experience that comes along.

6 Fate line starts close to the mount of Venus

You prefer to stay close to home and will probably do what is expected of you for most of your life. You feel obliged to work in the family business or follow a career that one of your parents has decided was right for you.

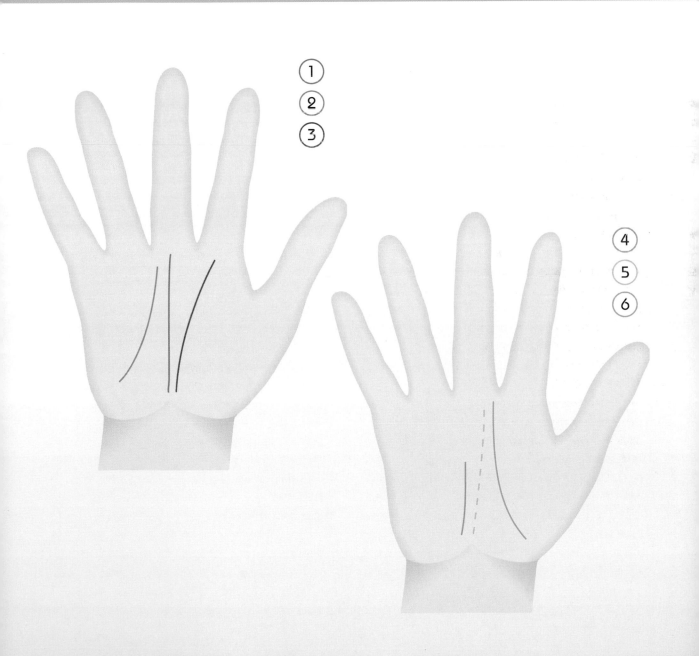

Practical palm-reading

There are two schools of thought concerning which hand means what. Some palm readers believe that your writing hand is the only hand you need to look at, while others think they are both of equal significance. I believe that the hand you write with is your 'main' hand.

Your potential

Your 'main' or major hand tells you about your conscious nature – in other words, how you behave and react; the kind of things in life that will make you feel good to be you; your life journey as it unfolds, and the events, influences and experiences in your life, past, present and future. The other hand, the one you don't write with, or minor hand, is also highly revealing, because it can show the unconscious, unawakened part of yourself; the potential you have inside you; your hidden talents and goals; what you really want and what it is possible to have.

Remember, the lines on your hands alter as you age, reflecting changing external events, unconscious desires or available potentials in your life.

Preparation

Be systematic. Don't try to read your whole palm in one session; or you will only get confused. Remember that the objective interpretations and meanings given above are only pointers to a more detailed analysis. Try to merge these signposts with your own intuitive powers and desires for the future.

You will probably find some contradictions as you interpret different aspects of your hand. This is quite normal, because as human beings we are full of contradictions. Your hand is an extension of your mind and a blueprint of who you are.

First, do this preliminary exercise.

- Write your name, address and favourite things by hand on a piece of paper. Don't think about it as you do so.
- Next, do the same thing and watch your hands move, as if you are observing yourself from outside yourself. This is the objectivity you need to cultivate when reading your hand, or when using any other divinatory tool for determining your future. If you project your fears, worries and desires onto your hand, you will not get a clear picture of what's going on.
- Touch your writing hand with your other hand. Does it feel soft, smooth, rough, bumpy, fleshy, hard, cold or hot? What does that make you think or feel? Do you like it?
- Now think what kind of hand you would like to have, if you don't like your own hand. If you wish you had a thinner one, warmer one, bigger one (or whatever), this reveals that you are probably not happy with the way you live your life, and now is the time to start making decisions and being honest with yourself about what you want for the future.
- Next, you have to be highly objective about reading your own hand. As human beings, we naturally tend to concentrate on the positive and ignore the negative aspects. However, any negative traits are very revealing and, with the right knowledge, you can turn them into positive attributes.

The reading

LIFE DIRECTION

If you have a large issue or problem concerned with your career or general life direction, look first at the shape of your major hand and decide whether it's a fire, air, earth or water hand (see pages 62–63). Are you following the directions outlined above? Next, look to the life, head and fate lines (see pages 68–69 and 72–75) for further information about your life direction.

RELATIONSHIPS

Focus on the shape of your major hand first, then look to the heart line (see pages 70–71), to determine what kind of relationships suit you best and how you express your emotional needs. Do you feel this describes you? If you agree, look at your minor hand: is the heart line slightly different and does it reveal something about yourself that you didn't know or weren't conscious of?

If you disagree with the interpretation of your main hand, you may be denying the qualities that it describes or are unaware that that's how you behave in relationships.

TALENTS AND TEMPERAMENT

If you're unsure about your natural talents or want more information about your temperament, look at the shape of your whole hand first, then at the mounts (if any are prominent, see page 66), and then at your fingers (see pages 64–65) to give you further information. Next, check out your head, fate and life lines.

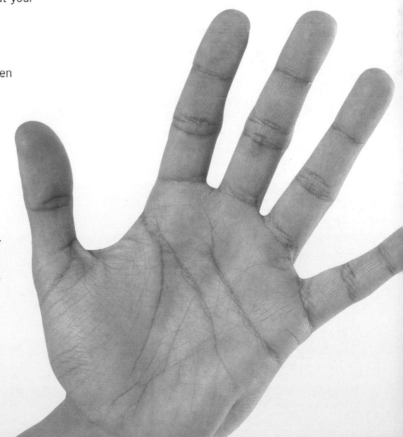

Drawing conclusions

As you read and observe, make notes. Jot down both negative and positive qualities – and don't cheat! What you're reading is a map of yourself. Build up the images, draw a picture of your hand and write keywords by each line or dominating feature, as in the example below.

These keywords will give you important ideas concerning your next steps and what the future holds. It's now up to you to express those potentials, make decisions and take responsibility for your future. Armed with this new self-awareness, you can fulfil those dreams or desires that are within reach. If you believe that life is simply fated, then of course it will oblige and external events will always influence you. But if you believe in making choices, instigating change and taking responsibility for your own future, then you will be in charge of your destiny.

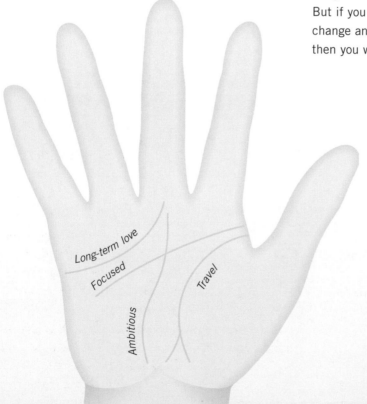

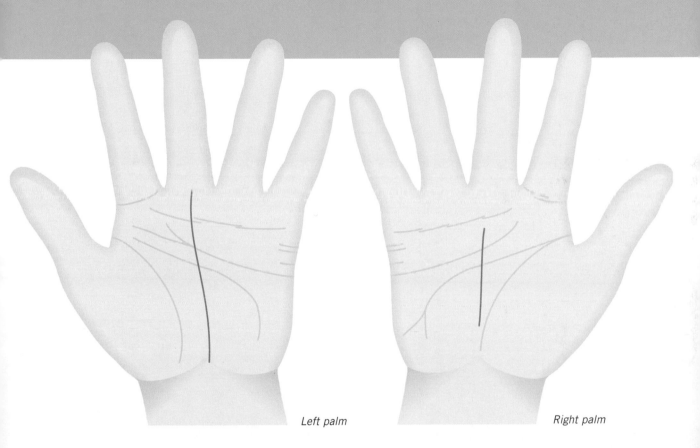

Left palm   *Right palm*

The minor hand

Your 'minor' hand will reveal your limitations, as well as possibilities and potentials that are hidden. Again, look at the overall shape of your hand. It's probably very similar to your main hand, but if there are any discrepancies, make a note of the difference. And likewise with the fingers and thumb.

The lines are most likely to reveal some interesting differences. Perhaps you have a rather faint, short fate line on your major hand, suggesting that you're not very ambitious or clear of your direction; you want to progress, but feel held back. On the minor hand the fate line may be longer and far more prominent, indicating that you need to express your individual desires and find a sense of vocation.

Unfortunately, this book isn't long enough to give you all the possible combinations, but armed with this small amount of knowledge you can start to reveal the direction of your own future and make your dreams come true.

RUNES

4 • RUNES

The runes are ancient Viking symbols, carved into rock, stones, pebbles or wood, and were primarily used to invoke the power of the gods. Norsemen believed that runes engraved on an object endowed it with magical power.

What can runes reveal about your future?

Runes – like crystals and all natural things – vibrate to a universal energy. When you use runes you are tapping into the harmonious vibrations of the universe for an answer.

Whenever you have to make a decision or have a question for which you can find no solution, consult your runes. They will give you a fresh perspective and tell you how best to act accordingly. The runes are objective and, like any oracle, give you great insights into yourself and your future intentions. Knowing what you really want, where you are going in life and what your personal journey is all about will be revealed by casting the runes at any moment of time. You can also use the runes as a meditational tool, or combine them with the I Ching or Tarot for in-depth readings.

The benefits of casting the runes
- Great for instant decision-making.
- Know what you truly want.
- Get solutions to questions.
- Gain the confidence to follow up on your real needs.
- Work on your self-development.
- Increase your sense of responsibility for making choices.
- Gain an objective viewpoint.
- Create balance and harmony in your life.

An ancient stone carved with magical runic script.

The history and language of runes

The word 'rune' originates from the Gothic word *runa*, meaning 'a secret thing or mystery'. The divinatory use of runes dates back thousands of years, but no one really knows when they first made their appearance in Europe. Originally they were a mysterious, magical system of symbols and glyphs, which represented the forces of nature; similar pictorial symbols carved onto rocks in Sweden date from 1300 BCE. The distinctive glyphs were also used among the Germanic peoples as signs and omens of fortune and empowerment.

There are 24 runes, divided into three groups of eight, which form the basis of the Viking alphabet. Each group was credited with special powers and was named after one of the Norse gods – Freyr, Hagal and Tyr. Runes were cast by tribes, cults and individuals, both as an oracle and to tell fortunes until the 11th century. This book uses the most popular surviving runic form, the 24 Norse runes, together with the mysterious blank rune, Wyrd, which was introduced at a later date. 'Wyrd' was the collective term for the three Norse sisters who represented 'All Knowledge', and are similar to the three Fates in Greek mythology.

The Runic Alphabet

A	B	C/K/Q	D	E	F	G	H	I	J/Y	L	M
ᚠ	ᛒ	ᚲ	ᛗ	ᛖ	ᛗ	ᚠ	ᚷ	ᚺ	ᛁ	ᛋ	ᛙ

N	O	P	R	S/Z	T	U	V/W	X/Th	Z	NG
ᛏ	ᛟ	ᚱ	ᚱ	ᛋ	ᛏ	ᚢ	ᛈ	ᚦ	ᛉ	◇

Making your own runes

The best way to get to know the runes is to make your own set. The time and effort involved empowers them not only with their ancient symbols, but also with your own life-force. So when you cast your runes, you are drawing on the universal energy that flows through you.

Using natural materials

The easiest way to make runes is to draw them on paper or cardboard and cut them out in the shape of stones. However, I strongly recommend using natural materials, which vibrate to the rhythms of universal energy.

The simplest set of natural runes can be made from flat stones or pebbles. These are everywhere: in your garden, in the countryside, in streams and on the beach. If you can't get to a beach, go to a fast-moving stream or a river; don't forget that you can now buy bags of pebbles and stones in many shops.

The ancient rune masters believed that if you take from nature, you must give something back, so if you do choose stones from a beach, stream or garden, leave a magical offering such as a sprinkling of sea-salt or some rice grains to replace the natural energy you have taken.

Collect about 30 stones, all of a similar size and shape (keep some spare, in case you ever lose one). Ideally, choose smooth and fairly flat stones. Copy the runic inscriptions (see pages 90–101) in acrylic or oil paint in a natural colour such as yellow ochre

or burnt sienna, depending
on the colour of the stones
and your personal preference.
It is important to leave one
stone blank. Varnish them
afterwards for protection.

The bag

You will need a bag or pouch
in which to keep the runes.
Use a piece of natural fabric such as silk, cotton,
linen or leather. Either tie the bag up with a string
or use a silk ribbon. Alternatively, use a favourite
old square scarf: fold the four corners of the scarf
together, then tie it with twine, string or ribbon.

The cloth

Finally, you need a rune cloth on which to cast your
runes. Again, use natural fabric (as above) and make
sure that your cloth is big enough to lay out all your
runes – about 45 x 45 cm
(18 x 18 in).

Empowering your runes

- First, charge the runes with your own vibrations by
  carrying them around with you for a whole day and
  putting them under your pillow or mattress at night.
- Next, use the following traditional method to
  empower the runes with natural energy.
- Lay out your runes on the casting cloth in the
  midday sun for an hour.
- At night leave them face-up on a window-ledge when
  there is a waxing or full moon (it doesn't matter if
  there is cloud cover).
- Write the runic alphabet on
  a piece of paper and either
  bury it in the garden or
  burn it on a fire.
- Your runes are now activated
  and ready for use.

Getting to know the runes

First, look at the images of the runes on pages 90–101: they are called 'upright' runes. But, if you turn them upside-down, most of them look very different – these are called 'reversed' runes. There are several runes that look the same whichever way up you place them.

Phrasing questions

To familiarize yourself with the runes, take one from your bag and look at it. Ask yourself what it means to you. Does it stir up any ideas, images or emotions? Do you like it, hate it, fear it, or simply fail to have an opinion about it? Now check the interpretation guidelines (see pages 90–101) to see what your rune means.

Make sure you always ask positive questions when consulting the runes. For example, if you are having a relationship problem, don't ask, 'Why is this relationship going wrong?' Instead, ask, 'What can I do to improve this relationship?'

You can also ask the runes to show you future potential. For example, 'What do I need to do to get that job' or 'What will be the outcome if I leave home and move to another country?' If you're confused, say, 'What do I need to do to be focused?' rather than, 'Why am I confused and don't know what to do?'

Working with a daily rune

To get you started, use the runes each day. Shake the bag gently, empty your mind and ask the runes to be your guide for the day ahead. Pick out a single rune from the bag and think about what it means to you. Then look up the interpretation to see what kind of day you can expect. If it's a reversed rune, don't assume that it's going to be bad day. Perhaps there's something lacking in your life that you need to explore? Throughout the day observe events, conversations and the energy in relation to the rune.

Two methods of casting the runes

There are many different ways to cast runes. You need to establish a ritual to aid your concentration, intuition and interpretation. In addition to the methods described below, runes may also be taken randomly from the bag and put into layouts, which are described at the end of this chapter (see pages 102–105). You can also use various tarot spreads or invent your own layouts when you become more proficient in rune interpretation.

CASTING METHOD 1

- Prepare your rune cloth. Lay it out on a flat table, or on the floor if you prefer to sit cross-legged in a meditative pose.
- Ask your question and concentrate hard.
- Without looking, remove from your bag five runes that feel as if they are 'speaking' to you and scatter them onto the cloth. If any runes fall beyond the cloth or just on the edge of it, ignore them. Those that are left on the cloth are the ones to work with.
- Turn up any runes that have fallen symbol-side down – unless, of course, it's the blank rune, Wyrd.
- Now interpret the runes in relation to your question and the relevant interpretations.

CASTING METHOD 2

- Prepare your rune cloth. Lay it out on a flat table, or on the floor if you prefer to sit cross-legged in a meditative pose.
- Ask your question and concentrate hard
- This time hold the bag in one hand, shake it gently and then scatter all the runes onto the cloth. Again, ignore any that are on the edge of the cloth or fall beyond it.
- Turn face-down any runes that are symbol-side up. Gradually pass your hands over the runes. Then turn over any rune that 'speaks' to you. For a beginner, I recommend choosing three runes at the most and interpreting these first. The more upright runes you have, the more immediately the decision or action will occur. If you have no upright runes, it simply means that any solution (however obvious) will be delayed for a while.

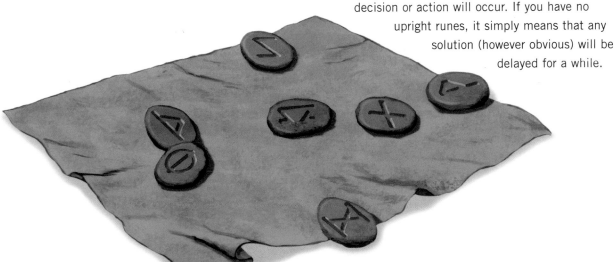

Reading the runes

Use the chart below for quick identification. As you become familiar with the symbols, open your mind to other ideas associated with the keywords. Reversed runes aren't always negative; they simply give you a different viewpoint, usually concerning what may be lacking.

Rune names and keywords

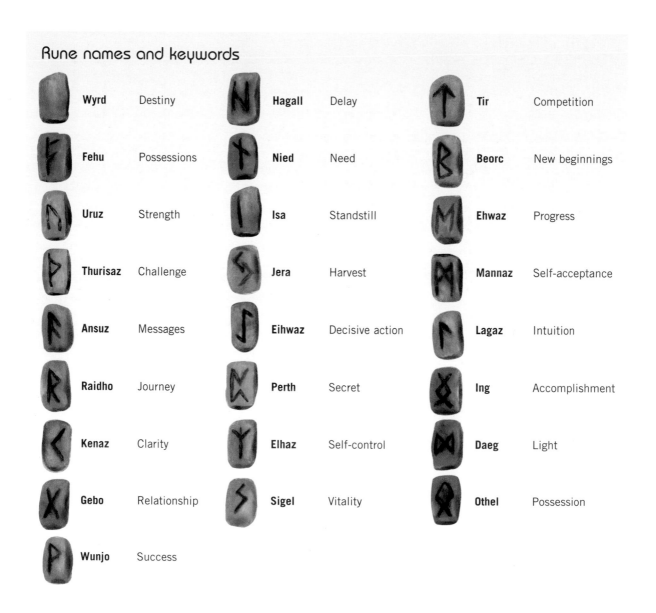

Rune	Name	Keyword
	Wyrd	Destiny
	Fehu	Possessions
	Uruz	Strength
	Thurisaz	Challenge
	Ansuz	Messages
	Raidho	Journey
	Kenaz	Clarity
	Gebo	Relationship
	Wunjo	Success
	Hagall	Delay
	Nied	Need
	Isa	Standstill
	Jera	Harvest
	Eihwaz	Decisive action
	Perth	Secret
	Elhaz	Self-control
	Sigel	Vitality
	Tir	Competition
	Beorc	New beginnings
	Ehwaz	Progress
	Mannaz	Self-acceptance
	Lagaz	Intuition
	Ing	Accomplishment
	Daeg	Light
	Othel	Possession

Meanings of the rune symbols

It takes practice to get to know the runes, so follow these interpretations to start with. To read the runes, use the keywords first and relate them to your question, followed by the longer interpretation. Eventually you will 'know' intuitively what each rune means.

Wyrd cast with Gebo signifies new love.

Wyrd and Raidho suggest a journey is imminent.

Wyrd
Destiny

This rune merits a whole page to itself, because it is the focal point for all the other runes. It has no number or symbol. It is blank, because you project all of your needs and desires into that blank space. Treat it as an empty place where you can sit awhile and meditate.

When cast with other runes, Wyrd signifies that what will be, will be. So look at the accompanying runes in your spread for clues. For instance, if Wyrd is accompanied by Gebo (Relationship), it's certain that new love is going to enter your life, whether or not you are searching for it. If you cast it with Raidho (Journey), the likelihood is that you will *have* to go on a journey, whether or not that is your intention.

Wyrd is neither negative nor positive. It can also signify that you are trying to discover something that is not meant to be known or not intended for you personally to know right now.

Wyrd is a complex rune. It asks you to consider whether you are in charge of your life. Destiny is when you make conscious decisions and take responsibility for your choices. Fate is when you feel that you are powerless to make choices. How do you want your life to be?

Fehu

Possessions

Signifies prosperity and personal possessions. But consider the price you have to pay for getting what you want. Material fulfilment is great, but remember to share your good fortune with others. Fehu also asks you to think about what you truly value. Are your values really your own or have you adopted someone else's values?

Uruz

Strength

You can overcome any obstacle. Uruz is a rune of vitality and changing situations. But you don't have to be passive. With courage and personal integrity, you can change the circumstances to suit you. It's time to put the past and its emotional baggage behind you, embrace change and live out your true potential.

Reversed Frustration and unfounded suspicions and doubts abound.

Reversed Self-doubt and fear are holding you back from reaching your true potential.

Thurisaz

Challenge

Don't act impulsively. Wait a little longer before making decisions. Thurisaz warns you not to assume that you know all the answers. Be cautious and objective. If you're looking for personal success, your intuition will signal when you're in the right place at the right time. When it does, go for gold.

Ansuz

Messages

Communications will help you pursue your dreams. Encounters with strangers may be the signposts to future happiness. Talk, learn and listen to gain wisdom. But also expect the unexpected. A surprise offer may change your life for the better.

Reversed Self-deceit is evident; you regret making a hasty decision.

Reversed Someone has selfish interests at heart and is not to be trusted.

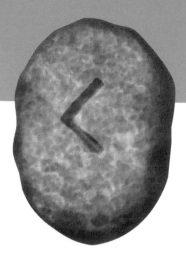

Raidho

Journey

Travel is favoured and may be physical, mental, emotional or spiritual. Set off in a new direction to discover more about yourself and the wider world. Raidho asks you to widen your perception through ideas, places and other people. Don't fear the unknown. Make your life journey what you want it to be, not what others think it should be.

Kenaz

Clarity

This creative rune helps you to see more clearly who you are in relation to others. Kenaz reveals that passion is important to you now. Your sexual and emotional happiness is at stake, so be honest about what you want. The truer you are to your own individuality, the better your relationships will be.

Reversed There are too many life choices; you can't decide which direction to take.

Reversed Don't be seduced by old ways; look for new ones.

Gebo

Relationship

Signifies success in every type of relationship. A commitment can now be made. New romance, profitable business ventures and all kinds of partnerships are favoured. Gebo reminds you that the best relationships are ones in which you honour each other's needs and accept that you are both separate individuals.

Wunjo

Success

A 'lucky' rune. It favours creative work, children, love, professional progress and material gain. But don't expect happiness to fall from the sky. Your skill, effort, willingness, character and optimism are the keys to personal joy. Don't give up on who you are; your true potential is about to shine through.

Reversed This rune is never reversed.

Reversed You aren't sure of yourself; you feel others can't trust you.

Hagall

Delay

Hagall reminds you that there will be delays to your plans. There are challenges ahead, but these are simply stepping stones to realizing your goal. The things you want now will come to you, but be prepared for other people, events or circumstances to get in your way. With perseverance you will succeed.

Nied

Need

Are you ignoring your needs for the sake of others? Is what you want incompatible with what you need? With self-awareness you can begin to accept that change is necessary in life to show you what your real needs are. Are your true sexual or emotional needs being met or are you just playing a game for fear of being rejected?

Reversed This rune is never reversed.

Reversed You are too needy right now; self-value and self-worth are lacking – don't give in to self-sabotage.

Isa

Standstill

You seem to be in limbo – as if time has stood still and you can't move forward or back. This rune can signify coldness in relationships or a lack of accomplishment. It's time to take a review of what's going on in all areas of your life. Pause, reflect, put your plans on hold. Prepare for the future and don't dwell on the past.

Jera

Harvest

It's up to you to reap the rewards of all your efforts. In the future there will be plenty more opportunities coming your way, as long as you prepare right now. As with any harvest, you must work hard. Water your ideas, cultivate your confidence and nurture your skill. Then there will soon be celebration and joy in your life.

Reversed This rune is never reversed.

Reversed This rune is never reversed.

Eihwaz

Decisive action

To make progress you have to take decisive action now. Don't put off the chance to change your life. Foresight and caution are valuable qualities, but so is the ability to embrace change, rather than fear it. Eihwaz also gives you the chance to uncover the truth about hidden secrets, especially if it's paired with Ansuz.

Perth

Secret

Known as the 'mystery rune', Perth indicates that it's time to uncover the truth. Take charge of your destiny rather than believing that it's in the hands of fate. No one can force you to do anything, unless you choose to let others do so. This rune also indicates 'sexual compatibility' if it falls with Uruz, Gebo or Wunjo. If you draw this as a solitary rune, it implies that a secret is about to be revealed.

Reversed This rune is never reversed.

Reversed Let go of the past; don't live by other's expectations. You doubt your ability to make the right choice, so make one now and be empowered.

Elhaz

Self-control

This rune signifies that you are about to go through a period of fortunate new influences. A new friendship, love interest or professional relationship could develop. You feel in control of your life, but don't become complacent.

Sigel

Vitality

A rune of success. You now have the power to effect changes in your life. Although you have bags of energy, you might think you can achieve more than you actually can. If you are concerned about your health, Sigel indicates vitality, youthfulness and rejuvenation of mind, body and spirit.

Reversed You feel vulnerable and your intuition isn't working well; be aware that there are people who could take advantage of your good nature.

Reversed This rune is never reversed.

Tir

Competition

If you are seeking career advancement, you can now make rapid progress. Your motivation and spirit will bring you success in any endeavour. If you have a love issue, this rune indicates positive passion and fiery feelings. A new lover is signified if you're looking for romance, but watch out for rivals.

Beorc

New beginnings

Declutter your heart. It's time to drop emotional baggage and let go of past regrets. You can now start afresh. This rune always indicates the birth of something – whether it's a new you, a love affair or a child of the mind or body. Nurture your ideas and get cracking.

Reversed You lack initiative – unlock your true potential and fight for what you believe in. In love issues, don't wear your heart on your sleeve.

Reversed You can't free yourself from the past, but you know it's time to move on; what are your own true values?

Ehwaz

Progress

All kinds of journeys or adventures are signified by this rune. You are either about to move home, change your long-term plans or shift your perspective. You have no choice but to get up and go. Just don't let pride get in the way of your true purpose.

Mannaz

Self-acceptance

Listen to what others have to say. Advice or objective interaction will open you up to a new way of looking at life. Take responsibility for your life and don't just drift along on the tide. Accept who you are – not what you think you should be.

Reversed You are static, unable to move on for fear of what others might think; make new contacts and remember to welcome adventure, rather than fear it.

Reversed People just don't seem to be on your wavelength; maybe you're not being totally honest about what you really want.

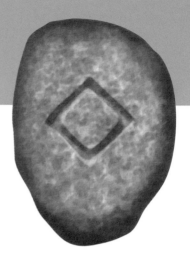

Lagaz

Intuition

The tide is now turning in your favour, but trust your intuition and remember to stay in touch with your inner voice. It's time to move on and not fear change. If this rune is cast with Mannaz, a psychic friend has some wonderful news for you.

Ing

Accomplishment

You can now achieve what you want and this rune indicates successful conclusions. Ing can signify a milestone opportunity coming your way, which will change your life for the better, such as a new job (with Fehu) or a new love affair (with Gebo or Wunjo).

Reversed Concentration is needed to sort out what is real and what is a flight of fancy. Learn to go with the flow rather than resist it.

Reversed This rune is never reversed.

Daeg

Light

A positive rune, which indicates that whatever you do now will bring you happiness, as long as you believe in yourself. You have vision and foresight, and know the best way to handle affairs. The sun is shining on you now. Make a new start and turn your dreams into reality.

Othel

Possession

Money can buy you lots of things, but it doesn't necessarily make you happy. Financial benefit could come to you now, but your values in love, work, friendship and lifestyle are in question. Othel indicates that you must focus carefully on what you want and, more importantly, why.

Reversed This rune is never reversed.

Reversed You may be too dependent on material wealth; in personal issues you can't buy your way out of a difficult situation – it won't make someone truly love you.

Rune layouts

You can use the runes for layouts, just as you use the Tarot for spreads. Here are four easy rune layouts to help get you started. Once you are more familiar with the runes, you can create your own layouts.

One-rune layout

This is the simplest layout and, rather like picking a rune for the day, it gives you a quick answer to any specific question. You can also ask an open-ended question, such as 'What do I need to know about myself?'

- Simply find a quiet place, shake your bag of runes, take one rune out and place it symbol side-up on the cloth.
- Before you lay the rune down, focus on your question. Here are a few examples of the kind of questions you could ask:
  'What issue is it important for me to focus on right now?'
  'What is stopping me from moving on?'
  'What is he thinking about me right now?'

Alternatively, you may just want a 'Yes' or 'No' answer to a simple question, such as:
'Does she love me?'
'Do I love him?'
'Are we right for each other?'
'Will I get the job?'
'Have I made the right decision?'
'Should I leave my partner?'
'Should I quit my job?'

- No matter which rune you pick, if it's upright the interpretation is 'Yes', and if it's reversed the answer is usually 'No'. However, you can use the issue, direction, outcome layout (see page 103) to confirm the answer. For an open-ended question, look at the interpretation for the relevant rune, which will lead you to the answer.

Yes   No

Issue, direction, outcome layout

This is a more detailed, but still simple, layout.
Use it to find out what is going on in your life right
now and how to deal with it.

- Relax and perform your opening ritual. Focus on
  your question.
- Select three runes and place them in front of you
  on your rune cloth, in the order shown below: each
  rune is turned face-up and interpreted in turn from
  left to right.

1 Issue
2 Direction
3 Outcome

HOW TO INTERPRET THE LAYOUT

- The first rune indicates the issue in question.
- The middle rune tells you which direction you must
  take regarding the issue.
- The last rune tells you the outcome of the issue.

EXAMPLE: **How should I progress in my career?**

1 Issue – Sigel: You're trying to achieve too much;
  you've bags of energy, but don't overdo it.
2 Direction – Elhaz, reversed: Don't deceive yourself.
  There are people out there who will take advantage
  of your vitality. Relax.
3 Outcome – Ehwaz: It's time to move on. Adventure
  beckons, so welcome it.

If you are honest with yourself, as Elhaz suggests,
and don't fall into the trap of believing everything
you hear, you will progress in a better direction.
The runes simply help you to make your life more
fortunate, rather than assume that your life is fated.

1

2

3

Destiny layout

Use this spread when you want guidance in dealing with current problems or issues and need to know the immediate and long-term outcomes.

- Relax and perform your opening ritual. Focus on your question.
- Select four runes and place them in front of you on your rune cloth, in the order shown right. In this layout they represent the energy of earth, water, fire and air respectively.

1 Practical results/challenges
2 Emotional lessons or tests
3 Personal destiny
4 Where to seek knowledge for future happiness

HOW TO INTERPRET THE LAYOUT
- Each rune represents one aspect of your destiny.

EXAMPLE: **I want a career change, but feel stuck at a crossroads.**

1 Practical results/challenges – Othel: The challenge right now is to ask yourself if you want to change direction simply for materialistic gain or for a real sense of vocation?

2 Emotional lessons or tests – Tir: You can now make rapid progress, but both your motivation and spirit will be tested. The lesson you learn from the runes is to be a warrior for your own cause and yours alone.

3 Personal destiny – Ansuz: Your personal destiny will be decided when a surprise offer changes your life for the better.

4 Where to seek knowledge for future happiness – Raidho: Wisdom and greater insight into your long-term future can be found by travelling, whether it comes through conversations with your travel companions or the strangers you encounter on the road. Go on holiday to work things through or involve yourself in work that means you will be travelling.

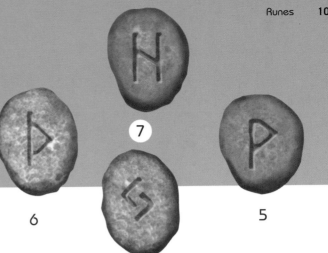

Tree of Life layout

The Tree of Life is one of the oldest and most sacred symbols in the world. This layout reveals deeper levels of understanding about who you are and what the outcome of your current desires and needs will be.

- Relax and perform your opening ritual. You don't need to ask a question with this spread.
- Select seven runes and place them in front of you on your rune cloth, in the order shown right.

1 What you need to learn
2 What will challenge you
3 Which rune can guide you
4 The power that will help you
5 What to avoid
6 What to let go of
7 The outcome of this knowledge

HOW TO INTERPRET THE LAYOUT

- Each rune represents one aspect of your life journey.

EXAMPLE

1 What you need to learn – Beorc: Let go of the past and accept that this is a time of new beginnings.
2 What will challenge you – Lagaz reversed: Your imagination will challenge you. Concentration is needed to sort out what is real and what is fanciful.
3 Which rune can guide you – Elhaz: You are about to go through a period of fortunate influences and a new friendship or love interest could develop.

4 The power that will help you – Jera: The seeds of ideas and your creative potential for growth will help you. Cultivate your confidence and nurture your skill.
5 What to avoid – Wunjo: Although this is a lucky rune, avoid thinking that happiness will simply fall from the sky. Your skill, willingness and optimism are the keys to personal joy.
6 What to let go of – Thurisaz: Let go of the assumption that you know all the answers. Be cautious and objective in every dealing.
7 The outcome of this knowledge – Hagall: The things you want will come to you in their own good time, even though other people or circumstances will get in your way. With perseverance and patience you will succeed.

READING AURAS

5 • READING AURAS

The word 'aura' comes from the Greek word for air. The aura is your personal energy, which consists of electromagnetic particles radiating from the body in many layers. This auric field is expressed by every living thing.

What can aura reading reveal about your future?

Your aura is your life-force and describes the state of your body, mind, spirit and soul. In historical art, the aura was often depicted as a halo around the head, but in fact the aura emanates all around you, particularly from the special energy fields of the body known as chakras. The aura is made up of many colours, which change with your moods, thoughts and feelings.

Reading your own aura is a positive method of self-development and insight into the future. You can begin to make choices for yourself and understand how other people's auras might inhibit, attract or overpower you. When you know the dominant colour of your aura, you are in a position to make personal inner changes or alterations to your own energy; you can find out your current secret desires and act upon them; you can decide to be more compassionate,

less critical or more confident. Loving your aura means that you are also learning self-love. And with self-love you can work towards making the future a time of happiness and personal fortune.

The benefits of reading your aura

- Find out your secret desires.
- Discover what energy you exude right now and how to make the most of it in the future.
- Develop greater self-esteem and self-love.
- Develop your ability to sense other people's auras, so that you know what to expect in relationships.
- Reveal which qualities you are lacking and which can be developed.

The aurora borealis is one of nature's extraordinary electromagnetic phenomena.

Aura history

The aura was described by Indian and Chinese mystics as long ago as 4000 BCE, and was often known as 'chi' or 'prana' And the interaction of colour and the human electrical field has been used for healing purposes since the time of ancient Egypt in the 6th century BCE. Pythagoras, the Greek philosopher and mathematician, used musical vibrations and colour to heal people.

Many people have seen the aura. The most famous was Nostradamus, the 16th-century astrologer and physician, who claimed to see the aura of a monk and correctly predicted that one day that monk would become Pope Sixtus V. In nature, the 'aurora' is a luminous meteoric phenomenon with electrical qualities, seen near the North and South Poles.

Despite the mystical nature of human auras, they have fascinated doctors and scientists for thousands of years. Paracelsus, one of the key figures in medical science in the 16th century, believed that a vital life-force emanated from the human body. The first person to succeed in taking a photograph of the aura was a Croatian engineer, Nikola Tesla, in the 1890s. He was followed by Semyon and Valentina Kirlian (after whom the technique of Kirlian photography was named) in the 1930s. More recently, an inventor called Guy Coggins developed an aura-imaging technique in 1980 and the aura-imaging camera is now one of the most popular ways to see your own aura at any given moment of time.

A Tibetan wall painting of Buddhist deities displaying their auras.

Auras and the chakras

Many Eastern traditions maintain that energy flows through the body, linked by energy centres, or chakras, which are associated with particular colours. As your physical, emotional or mental state changes, the colours of the chakras vibrate and hence your aura alters.

Awakening your chakra energy

Try this simple exercise to awaken your chakra energy and balance your aura. Move your hands very slowly over each chakra area (see the illustration), about 5 cm (2 in) away from your body. Think of the associated colour as you hold your hands still over each chakra area and imagine that you're radiating only that colour. Does it feel good, uncomfortable or indifferent? If you feel good about that colour, you're expressing it well. If you feel uncomfortable or indifferent, then you need to work on the qualities associated with that colour, to help improve your lifestyle and future happiness.

Looking after your aura

To take care of your aura, first perform a 'massage'. Without actually making contact with your body, place your hands together, forming a cup. Start from your feet and slowly move your hands upwards, as if you were massaging your body in a sweeping movement, right up to the top of your head. Make the massage last for about three to four minutes. As you massage, do you feel different hot or cold spots? Does your aura feel soft, bumpy, smooth or ruffled in any way? Make a note of any places of discomfort or coldness, then check which is the nearest chakra. It is likely that the corresponding colour is blocked, so work to integrate the qualities of that colour into your life.

The position of the seven chakras and their corresponding aura colours.

Aura questionnaire

Before you use your aura to tell you about the direction of your future, you need to evaluate what state it is in. Is its energy balanced or does it need strengthening? Use this short questionnaire to determine the true state of your aura.

For every 'Yes' answer, score one point; then check the score totals for your aura evaluation.

	Yes	No
I attract people who end up hurting me.	☐	☐
I'm envious of my friends.	☐	☐
I get jealous if my partner talks to someone else.	☐	☐
I hate criticism.	☐	☐
My relationships are always complicated.	☐	☐
I don't find it easy to say no.	☐	☐
I don't feel comfortable in a strange place.	☐	☐
I'd rather watch television than do exercise.	☐	☐
I've got great ideas, but never do anything about them.	☐	☐
I get stressed out by other people's problems.	☐	☐
I feel scared of making my own decisions.	☐	☐
Traffic jams faze me.	☐	☐

Score totals

11+ Your aura needs strengthening.

8–11 Your aura needs a little more love and attention.

5–8 Your aura is in good shape, so keep it that way.

1–5 Your aura is vibrant and powerful – take good care of it.

Developing your aura

Now that you know the state of your aura, you can begin to develop it, using the techniques described below. Remember that your aura changes with you, so bear in mind that you will probably respond differently to these techniques if you do the same exercise every month.

Strengthening your aura

- Simply sit in a calm, relaxed atmosphere. Hold a piece of white quartz crystal in one hand and breathe deeply and slowly.
- Focus on your hand and the power of the crystal energy. Imagine your own auric energy merging with the crystal energy for two to three minutes, to restore your own life-force.
- Do this exercise every evening if you had a high score in the aura questionnaire (see page 111). Afterwards, tell yourself that your aura energy is harmonious and that you're going to take good care of it.

Enhancing your intuition

Often known as the 'sixth sense', gut instinct or psychic awareness, intuition is the key sense that tells you about your own and other people's auras. If you can sense the auras of those around you, you can tell whether you will have a good relationship with a stranger or potential partner; how to deal with people in professional situations; and whether you should approach people for work, get to know them on a social basis or trust them with your money. This means that you can safely make decisions about your future direction and involvement with others, based on their auric energy.

- You can do this visualization technique anywhere, but it's best to find a quiet place, alone.
- First, relax and breathe quietly for a few minutes; imagine yourself walking down a long road. Imagine where you have been, what you were doing before you reached this road and why you are there.
- Now you are in a beautiful landscape. To your left is a huge cave, where you decide to stop and rest for a while. In the cave is a golden chair, upon which you sit.
- A shaft of pure white light beams down upon the top of your head and you feel its energy

empowering you. Imagine the light reaching every part of your body, within and without. Let it rest in the area below your navel, known as the 'hara' – the centre of your life-force. Your own energy is literally being topped up.

- Now imagine that energy being any colour you want. If you feel passionate about life, you might imagine red, for example. Visualize the coloured light flowing through every cell of your body, then radiating beyond your body, outwards into the cave.
- Imagine that you stand up and walk out of the cave, with the colour still radiating from you as you walk down the road.

Extraordinary landscapes are in your mind, too.

- Now you meet a friend who has been to his or her own secret cave and you imagine what his or her aura colour is. Does it clash with yours? Do you wish you were radiating that colour or are you glad to have your own?
- Now turn away and, before you let go of the image, gently visualize your own aura at rest, but still radiating from your body. Use this technique to revitalize your own aura whenever you need to, and to increase your intuitive skills for reading other people's auras.

Seeing your own aura

You can literally learn to 'see' your own aura. This does take practice, but with the knowledge of your predominant aura colour, you will know how to make the most of your current strengths and qualities, in tandem with your future goals.

CANDLE PRACTICE

- Sit quietly in a darkened room one evening when there is no breeze.
- Light a candle and place it in front of you on a table.
- Concentrate on the candle flame and watch it flicker and burn. The less it moves, the better. Focus on the flame for a few seconds, and you will begin to see a glow around the flame with your peripheral vision.
- Try to imagine the colours of the candle's aura. Don't do this for longer than ten seconds or so, because it can tire your eyes.
- Think about which particular colour stands out for you; it's likely it represents a theme or quality which is important in your life right now or needs attention.

MIRROR PRACTICE

- Again, choose a quiet evening when you're feeling relaxed and a place where there is very low-key lighting. Make sure that no one will interrupt you.
- Sit in front of a mirror. Behind you on a table or ledge place a lighted candle, which cannot be seen in the reflection as you look at yourself, but creates a gentle glow behind you as you stare at your face in the mirror.
- Stare into your own eyes, relax and listen to your breathing; empty your mind of all thoughts, as if you were meditating.
- Depending on your ability to see auras, it could take a few minutes before you begin to perceive the glow of the candle around you illuminating your own aura. Remember, this takes practice and the image and colours will change according to your mood.
- Once you can see the aura that the candle creates around you, try doing the same exercise without the candle. Concentrate on your mirror image, and in a few minutes, through your peripheral vision, you will see and sense the radiance and colour of your aura.

Aura colours

The colours of your aura are vibrations of energy, swirling particles that are given off from the electro-magnetic charge of your energy field. They will tell you about your secret desires, how you can map out your own future and what you can hope to achieve. There are ten basic colours most likely to be seen in your aura:

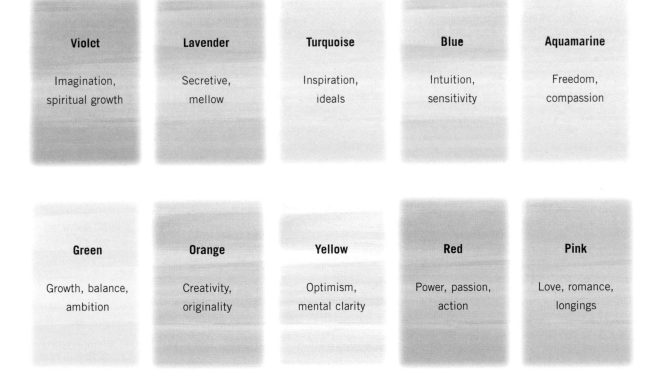

Violet

Imagination, spiritual growth

Lavender

Secretive, mellow

Turquoise

Inspiration, ideals

Blue

Intuition, sensitivity

Aquamarine

Freedom, compassion

Green

Growth, balance, ambition

Orange

Creativity, originality

Yellow

Optimism, mental clarity

Red

Power, passion, action

Pink

Love, romance, longings

Next, follow the steps overleaf to find out your dominant aura colour and to determine what your future potential needs and goals are.

How to find your dominant aura colour

As your moods, feelings and circumstances change, so does your aura. Here is a simple technique that you can use to discover which of the ten basic colours is currently most vivid in your aura.

- Read the keywords listed in the Mood column and rate each from 10 to 1. Give a score of 10 to the word you most easily identify with or believe you express right now. Rank all the other Mood keywords, down to a score of 1 for the quality you believe you express least. For example, you might give 10 to Secretive, 9 to Dreamy, 8 to Enthusiastic, 7 to Free and easy, and so on.
- Rank the keywords in the Feelings and Thoughts columns using the same technique.
- Now transfer your scores for each word to the colour chart on page 117. If you scored 10 for Ambitious in the Mood column, write 10 next to Ambitious in the green band of the colour chart.

Mood		Feelings		Thoughts	
Flirtatious	☐	Psychic	☐	Dynamic	☐
Playful	☐	Inspired	☐	Quick-witted	☐
Ambitious	☐	Unemotional	☐	Reflective	☐
Free and easy	☐	Calm	☐	Focused	☐
Extroverted	☐	Spontaneous	☐	Self-confident	☐
Diplomatic	☐	Sensitive	☐	Scattered	☐
Dreamy	☐	Vibrant	☐	Sexy	☐
Secretive	☐	Passionate	☐	Intuitive	☐
Frustrated	☐	Light-hearted	☐	Creative	☐
Enthusiastic	☐	Lucky	☐	Indecisive	☐

Do the same for each word, until you have recorded a score next to every word in the colour chart.

- Now add up the score for each aura colour. For example, for Violet add up the scores for Dreamy, Psychic and Reflective, and fill in the total at

the end. The colour with the highest total score is your dominant aura colour.

- If two or more colours have equal scores, close your eyes and visualize each colour in turn. Whichever colour it is easiest to 'see' is your main aura colour.

Aura colour	Mood		Feelings		Thoughts		Total
Violet	Dreamy		Psychic		Reflective		
Lavender	Secretive		Sensitive		Intuitive		
Turquoise	Frustrated		Inspired		Creative		
Blue	Diplomatic		Calm		Focused		
Aquamarine	Free and easy		Light-hearted		Indecisive		
Green	Ambitious		Unemotional		Self-confident		
Orange	Enthusiastic		Lucky		Quick-witted		
Yellow	Playful		Vibrant		Scattered		
Red	Extroverted		Passionate		Dynamic		
Pink	Flirtatious		Spontaneous		Sexy		

The aura colours

Now you can look up your dominant aura colour and discover both your future direction and your relationship potential.

- Use the quick guide below to discover the hidden message or secret of your dominant aura colour.
- Then turn to the profile for your dominant colour to see what it reveals about your 'Future direction'.
- Do the keywords test at regular intervals to see if you respond in the same way.

Dominant aura colour	Secret desire
Violet	Spiritual awakening
Lavender	Unconditional love
Turquoise	Lifestyle change
Blue	To find your true vocation
Aquamarine	Adventure
Green	Fame/prestige
Orange	Travel/fun
Yellow	Independence
Red	Financial success
Pink	New romance/partnership

Violet

Future direction You feel more compassionate than you've been for a long time and your thoughts are intuitive, so develop psychic connections with long-lost friends or relatives. Reflect carefully on your direction and connect with new friends involved in the alternative arts, which will be beneficial to your future happiness.

Relationship You need a partner who understands your ethereal moods and can bring you down to earth with a gentle bump. You prefer to idealize than accept the reality of human relationships. For good fortune in love, try to accept that no one is perfect. You will attract musicians, poets and spiritual gurus into your life, if you are single.

Lavender

Future direction Channel your compassion into helping others. Your thinking is clear, so make precise decisions and be inspired by your imagination. It's time to chill out, take long walks in the country or enjoy a laid-back attitude to life. Treasure your leisure time rather than worrying about the rat-race.

Relationship Your aura will attract easy-going, reliable people into your life. Right now you need a loving, caring relationship. If a partner or potential lover is stressed out, you will sense it deeply, so rather than repress your feelings, talk things through for mutual harmony.

Turquoise

Future direction Take a positive attitude to your own psychological growth, while you're spirited and creative. The future is certainly on your mind, so projects can now be developed positively. Opt for a relaxed social atmosphere out of work hours, and lots of physical exercise to channel your high energy levels. Communicate your ambitions and be rewarded.

Relationship Easy-going and romantic, you need a lover who is adventurous and good fun. Intellectual interaction and your own freedom are essential for personal growth. You can now make it clear to a current partner that your independence is important, too. If you're single, you will attract laid-back admirers with a good sense of humour into your life.

Blue

Future direction Your head and heart are in balance, so you will have good hunches that will pay off in the long-term. You're sensitive to the needs of others, yet positive and determined to succeed. You're ready for more responsibility and will soon take on all kinds of projects or develop important new strategies for achieving your life goals.

Relationship You need an intimate relationship right now. A creative partner will bring you the joy you're looking for, as long as you have a deep sexual rapport. If you're single, you will attract an intensely loyal admirer into your life. It will take time to get to know him or her, as he or she will have a suspicious nature.

Aquamarine

Future direction Your moods fluctuate between feeling vulnerable and carefree, yet you can organize your brilliant creative ideas and make them real. You are in transition and a career change is signified. With high energy levels and self-confidence you can make some very important decisions. The future is bright and breezy for you, so go with the flow.

Relationship You need a carefree, intellectually stimulating relationship. If you're attached, you are really in tune with your partner, but this is not the time to commit. Sex will be outrageous and fun. If you're single, you will attract equally fascinating, unpredictable characters into your world.

Green

Future direction Motivated and strong willed, you need prestige, fame or a goal to aim for. Work hard and promote your talents to those who can help you. With thoughts on how to make more money or improve your lifestyle, the future looks rosy if you stick to your chosen pathway.

Relationship You're determined to make a current love relationship work out in the long term. You have a down-to-earth attitude to love, sex and sensual pleasure, and will soon be settled in a mutually ambitious partnership. If you're single, you will attract financial whizz-kids, mature VIPs or wealthy benefactors.

Orange

Future direction Original and self-confident, you're going through a period of good luck. Now is the time to get on with all those projects you've been putting on the back-burner. You have a brilliant rapport with people and a natural flair for saying the right thing at the right time. So get out there and generate that natural spirit of optimism and you will be rewarded.

Relationship Right now you need loads of space. Extrovert and fun-loving, you adore mental stimulation with no emotional involvement. You're about to enjoy a madcap sexual phase. If you're looking for love – wild, adventurous partners will be attracted to your free-spirited aura.

Yellow

Future direction Enthusiastic and playful, you're curious about everyone and everything. Your ambitions are creative and your fun-loving attitude is contagious. Make your personal fortune by communicating all your ideas. Phone calls, emails and other transactions will bring some life-changing opportunities.

Relationship Your flirtatious aura will attract the opposite sex to you like moths to a flame. Tell any partner or new lover that you're more interested in fun than in being tied down. Challenges are coming your way, but they are the kind you like best: a romantic partner or a clandestine affair.

Red

Future direction Your dynamic and charismatic aura won't go unnoticed by anyone. You can do twice as much work as your colleagues and you're geared up to maximize your success. Get new ventures off the ground now, to achieve great fortune in the months to come. Passionate and driven, you can achieve anything you want.

Relationship Passion is your watchword and you're wild about sex. Fun-packed escapades are on the cards, and so is a demanding partner who can match your extremist nature. Wicked or taboo subjects will be raised in the future, so face up to them. If you're single, your aura will attract serial romantics and one-night standers – make sure you know which you want.

Pink

Future direction Concentrate on your future happiness, while sparkling ideas and loving thoughts dominate your mind. You're happy with your career right now, and your bubbly personality makes it easy for you to gain the upper hand in any business event. It's time to make a key decision and take responsibility for your choices.

Relationship You need a partner who can be as romantic and sexually creative as you. If you're attached, you won't feel ready to make a commitment. Falling in love with love means that you never really get to know the one you're with. Give it time. If you're single, light-hearted admirers will be attracted to your seductive aura.

PENDULUM DOWSING

6 • PENDULUM DOWSING

Pendulum dowsing uses a weight attached to a thread, chain or string to read universal energy patterns via your unconscious vibrational connection to the cosmos.

What can pendulum dowsing reveal?

You can use the pendulum to answer virtually any question and to reveal more about your own inner desires and feelings. But it's the way you ask questions that is important. It's no good asking, 'Should I go out with John or Michael?' or 'How could I improve my life?' The pendulum only answers, 'Yes', 'No', 'I don't know' and 'I don't want to answer'. So you can ask, 'Does John love me?', 'Does Michael love me?' and 'Will it be sunny on Saturday?' You can also ask, 'Am I really happy in this relationship?' and 'If I left the country to start a new life, would I be miserable?'

The benefits of pendulum dowsing

• Locate lost objects.
• Make decisions easily.
• Select a potential partner.
• Understand your unconscious desires.
• Ask Yes/No questions about the future.
• Evaluate a situation or a person.

The history of pendulum dowsing

The pendulum has been used for thousands of years as a magical device to reveal secret desires, find lost objects, determine the sex of unborn children and choose dates for special events. In ancient Egypt the pendulum was used to decide on the best place to grow crops, while the Romans were condemned for using it to plot against the emperor.

In the early 19th century an Italian, Francesco Campetti, used a pendulum to discover water and minerals underground, as did a French water diviner in the 1930s. Pendulums have also been used to locate hidden mines and underground tunnels in times of war, but are now more commonly used for personal discovery and fortune-telling. There is no limit to what the pendulum can tell you.

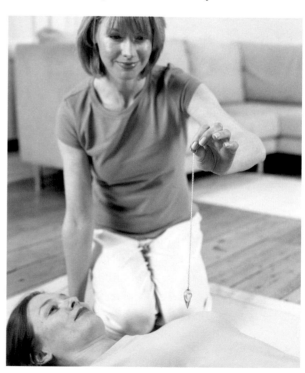

Pendulum dowsing has been used for centuries to determine the sex of an unborn child.

How does pendulum dowsing work?

Tiny, involuntary movements of the hand that holds the pendulum cause it to move. Cosmic energy patterns permeate your unconscious mind and it is these patterns that make the muscles react, without you realizing it. This is called the 'ideomotor response' and the pendulum simply amplifies these tiny movements.

The pendulum enables you to tap into the hidden knowledge that you carry deep within you. Whatever question you ask, the answer comes from the universal energy via your own unconscious mind. The best results occur when you are totally objective; if you ask questions about yourself, the pendulum may be influenced by your wishful thinking. Emotional involvement with the question can often override the true response, so be very honest with yourself before asking questions.

Choosing a pendulum

There are many different styles of pendulum available in New Age shops, particularly crystal ones, which carry their own natural energy. Opt for one that you like for its look and its weight when suspended between your finger and thumb. Round, cylindrical or spherical shapes are best, because they are symmetrical. You can even make your own pendulum using a paper clip or a ring suspended from a piece of thread. Here are four different types of pendulum shape that you might come across.

Pyramid

Cylindrical

Crystal

Mermet

How to use a pendulum

You can swing your pendulum from a sitting or standing position. The following instructions describe how to use it when sitting. If you prefer to stand, bend your arm at an angle of 90 degrees at your elbow, so that your forearm is parallel with the ground.

Pendulum dowsing instructions

- Sit down at a table and rest your elbow on it.
- Hold the end of the thread or chain of your pendulum between your thumb and first finger, using very little pressure. The pendulum should be hanging about 30 cm (12 in) in front of you.
- Make sure that your elbow is the only point of contact with the table.
- Do not cross your legs or feet, because this blocks the energy flow.
- Swing the pendulum in gentle circles to get used to the feel of it.
- Experiment with the length of thread to see whether a shorter or longer drop would work better for you.
- Once you feel comfortable with the swing and the drop, stop the movement with your other hand.
- Now put your first question: ask which movement indicates a 'Yes' response. You can say your question aloud or just think it; the pendulum will eventually respond and move in the direction that signifies 'Yes' (see right). If you have never used a pendulum before, it might take a while before it moves. Be patient. It might move just a tiny bit at first, but if you keep on thinking 'Yes', it will move more and more strongly.
- Sometimes you might have to try several times before you get a reaction. And the pendulum will work more fluidly if you're open, imaginative and willing to trust in the unconscious energies flowing through you. *Do not move your hand, arm or wrist!*

The kinds of swings and their different meanings

Your pendulum will move in one of four ways:

1 Backwards and forwards
2 From side to side
3 In a clockwise circle
4 In an anti-clockwise circle

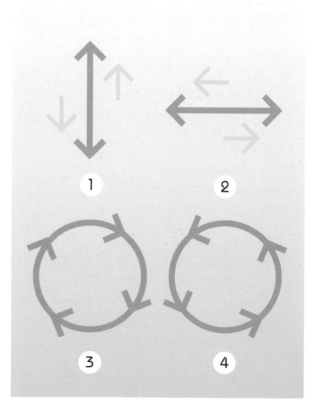

- The 'Yes' swing is not the same for everyone, which is why you have to find out which type of swing is positive for you. Some people discover that it's a clockwise swing, others from side to side, and so on. It's all a matter of personal vibration and your own connection to the unconscious.

- Next, ask which is a 'No' swing. Then ask which is the 'I don't know' swing and finally which swing signifies 'I don't want to answer.'

- Make a note of each swing, then follow the exercises below to reaffirm the swings and their different meanings.

- These responses should remain the same for the rest of your life. But do check again if you take a long break between using the pendulum, because you will have changed and so will your inner energy.

Questions to ask your pendulum to confirm Yes/No swings

To check the validity of the swing, first ask questions to which you already know the answers, such as, 'Is my name such and such?', 'Am I a woman?' Obviously, if you are female, the pendulum should answer 'Yes'; if you're male, 'No'. You can either ask these questions aloud or think them in your head.

Once the pendulum has confirmed questions to which you know the answers, you can ask questions to which you don't know the answers. This is when your unconscious starts to connect with the universal energy and generates the pendulum's response to your inner vibrational contact with the universe.

First of all, have fun asking questions. Ask questions that determine the best pathway to follow, such as, 'Should I stay in my current job rather than look for a new one?' If the answer is negative, then you can ask, 'Would I be better off in a different profession?' And so on. You can also ask questions about the future, such as 'Is this going to be a good day for me?' and 'Will John/Jane fall in love with me?' (Take care, with this sort of question, that you are not projecting your desires into the movement of the pendulum.)

Exercise to develop your abilities

Try this experiment to see how your conscious mind has power over the pendulum, too.

- Suspend your pendulum and keep it still with your free hand.
- When it's motionless, let go and ask the pendulum to move in a clockwise circle. *Do not move your hand, arm or wrist.* Concentrate on the pendulum, staring at it and thinking, 'Clockwise, clockwise.' You will find that in a few seconds the pendulum will move in that direction.
- Stop the pendulum and think about a different direction. You will find that once again it follows your thoughts.
- Now free yourself from the power of your conscious mind by focusing on the pendulum without thinking about it. Meditate on a question by repeating it over and over again, so that stray thoughts or feelings don't block the gateway between your conscious mind and the unconscious. With practice, you will learn to know the difference between your mind intentionally causing the pendulum to move in a particular direction and being open and receptive to the power of universal energy that you are seeking.
- The most important thing to remember is to trust in the power of the pendulum and believe that you are truly connecting to the realms of the unconscious. Practice, practice and practice again, always makes perfect.

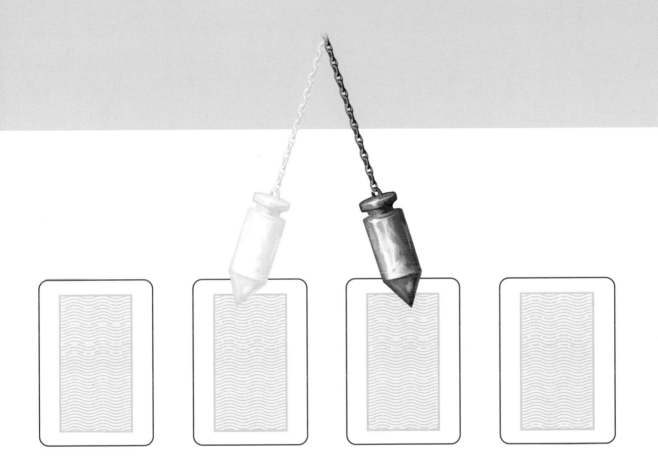

Card test

Now try this card test to see whether you have been able to relinquish conscious control.

- Make a random selection of four cards from a pack. Shuffle them thoroughly, then take the top card and look at it. This is going to be the card that your pendulum has to find: say you choose the Ace of Hearts.

- Mix and shuffle the four cards again, face-down, until you really don't know where the Ace is. Then lay them out face-down in a row in front of you.

- Ask the pendulum to find the card. Suspend it over each card in turn and ask, 'Is this the Ace of

Hearts?' Be patient if it takes a while to move and if it says, 'I don't know', try again. Give the pendulum time to move in a steady, sure direction.

- The pendulum should give you a negative response for three of the cards and a positive response over the Ace of Hearts. If it's wrong, you haven't quite got the confidence to let go of all conscious control. Again, practice will eventually make perfect.

Pendulum divining

Once you have mastered an unconscious connection, you can use a pendulum for all sorts of reasons: to find a lost object, to predict the future, to establish whether you will have a fruitful relationship with someone, and for greater self-knowledge.

To find an object

Practise this exercise by finding something that someone has hidden for you, such as a key, until you can do it without getting flustered. When you actually lose something, usually you have simply forgotten where you put it, which creates anxiety. With this test, you won't be panicking about whether you will actually find it or not.

- Stay calm and relaxed, and get a friend or partner to hide the object in your home.
- Ask the pendulum an obvious question first, such as, 'Is the key in the home?' This checks that the pendulum is working through you. A positive response will give you faith in its answers, too.
- Next, narrow down the search. Ask if the key is in the kitchen. Then ask the same for all the other rooms in your home, until you get a positive response from the pendulum.
- Once you know which room the key is in, ask precise questions like, 'Is the key in the laundry basket?' and 'Is the key under the carpet?' Usually by the time you have got this far you will spot the key or the pendulum will respond positively over a chest of drawers or the rug.

To predict the future

Your perception of the future is highly subjective. You have wishes, desires, needs and doubts that you project into the future. This means that you have to be very honest when using the pendulum to find out things about yourself. However, it can give you the courage to do something you really want to do or tell you whether the flat you intend to buy or the person you're about to marry will make you happy.

If you are about to go for a job interview, suspend the pendulum over the advertisement in the paper and ask, 'Will I be happy in this work?' Always ask questions that are specific. You can also ask the pendulum if someone will make a good friend or lover. After meeting them for the first time, ask questions such as, 'Are they trustworthy?', 'Are they loyal?' and 'Are they good for me?'

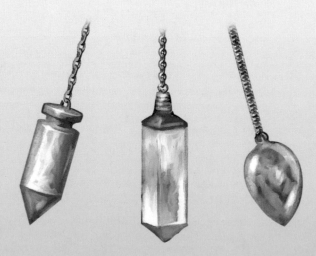

To test a relationship

To find out whether a particular relationship will be harmonious, try the following test.

- First, select two similar coins. Put them on the table a little way apart, then suspend your pendulum between the two coins. After a few moments the pendulum will begin to swing from side to side, from one coin to the other. This means that they are in harmony with each other – whether or not your personal positive response is from side to side, backwards and forwards or in a circular motion.

- Now replace one of the coins with a very different object, such as a wedding ring, pen or pack of cards. Again suspend the pendulum and this time you will find that it either stays still or moves backwards and forwards, avoiding the two items. This means that they are not in harmony. You can see by this that the pendulum reacts differently when two objects are the same and when they are different. You can now apply this method to people.

- Say you are about to go on a first date with someone and want to know whether or not you're going to get on. Write your names on two small pieces of paper, then place them on the table about 13 cm (5 in) apart and suspend the pendulum between them. It will either move from one to the other, indicating a harmonious relationship, or will stay still or even move away from the paper, indicating a difficult first date.

Dowsing for self-knowledge and self-improvement

You can also use the pendulum to ask questions about yourself. But do take care, because you may get the answer you want to receive, rather than the whole truth. You must be very honest (no cheating hand movements, either) and clear all negative energies first, by means of cleansing rituals or meditation techniques. Try out this exercise to get to know your true nature. Then you can remedy anything that needs appropriate action.

Test statements

I am confident and motivated.

I deserve love just by virtue of being on this earth.

I am successful.

I am a good team player.

I am willing to help anyone.

I don't have any inhibitions.

I love my partner (if you are attached).

I'm happy being single (if you are single).

- Find a quiet place, clear your mind of negative thoughts and say the test statements (see below left) out loud, one by one, while you let your pendulum magic work.
- Close your eyes, repeat each statement a few times in your head or out loud, then see what your pendulum is doing. If it gives a positive response, you are living out that particular statement and are in harmony with it. If it gives a negative response, this area of your life needs improvement. For example, you may think that the statement 'I'm a confident person' is correct, but the pendulum might give a negative response. Follow up on this by asking a series of simple questions, such as, 'Am I confident when entering a room full of people?' and 'Do I like being the centre of attention?' With honest self-awareness you can become more confident or accept that this is an issue you need to work on in yourself.
- If the pendulum's response is indecisive, it is likely that you are not comfortable with that statement.

Wants and wishes list

The pendulum can also be used to help you achieve a goal, a desire or a dream (as long as it's realistic). But first you have to find out which desires are genuine and which are not important right now.

- Note all your wants and wishes on separate pieces of paper. For example:

I want to be a celebrity.

I want to be a millionaire.

I want to travel.

I want to have lots of friends.

I wish to have a beautiful home.

I wish for love.

I wish for good health.

I wish for a family.

I want to have perfect skin.

- Put your desires in order, with your greatest desire listed first.
- Suspend your pendulum over the first desire. Think about it for a while and what it would do for you. Would it change your life? Would other people love you more or less? Watch what your pendulum does. If it gives a positive movement, this desire is good for you; if negative, then it's not right to follow it up just now.
- Suspend your pendulum over each piece of paper in turn and make notes of the responses. You will probably find that you have one, two or three desires that are positive and the rest may be negative or 'don't knows'. Put those to one side and focus on one main goal.
- For the next few days suspend your pendulum over the final paper selected and make an affirmation aloud that you will do anything to achieve this goal. Your conscious mind is in tune with the unconscious energies at work in the cosmos. You can now work to make this a reality.

I CHING

7 • I CHING

The origins of the I Ching date back thousands of years to when Chinese fortune-tellers consulted patterns in nature, such as the lines on tortoise shells, to predict the future. This method of divination developed into an oracle called the 'Book of Changes' or I Ching.

The history of the I Ching

The first known development of the I Ching into a written work is attributed to the legendary first Emperor of China, Fu Hsi, who understood the basic patterns in nature underlying everything we do. Using this knowledge, he composed the eight three-lined glyphs, or 'trigrams', that form the basis of the I Ching. These eight trigrams represent the eight fundamental energies of nature, which permeate all human life.

Much later, in the 6th century BCE, the well-respected sage and philosopher Confucius redeveloped the whole system of the I Ching and it became an integral part of Chinese culture. It was not known in the West until the end of the 19th century, when a German missionary, Richard Wilhelm, translated the text into German. Not long afterwards, Carl Jung, the great psychologist, saw the I Ching as confirmation of his own theories about the synchronicity of events in life. Since then it has been widely used in the West as a wonderful tool for divination and fortune-telling.

The benefits of using the I Ching

- Find solutions to dealing with a certain problem.
- Get objective answers to direct questions.
- Get guidance when you are at a crossroads.
- Learn more about your own personal development.
- Discover the best way to act for the future.
- Get help in making choices.
- Get advice regarding the immediate outcome of a particular issue.

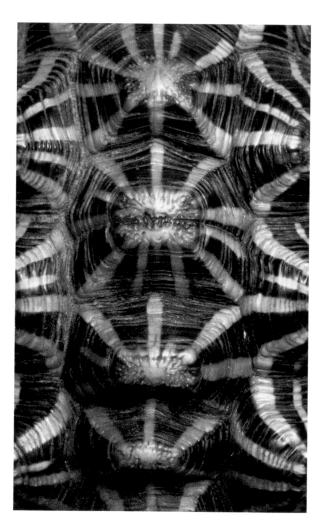

The intricate patterns on a tortoise shell were once used to predict the future.

Yin and yang

The symbols for yin and yang form the basis of the eight trigrams used in the I Ching and are symbols of all that happens, shifts and develops in your life. The origins of 'yin' and 'yang' are shrouded in mystery, but they simply represent two opposing energies: yang is summer, sunshine, heat, noise and light; yin is winter, the moon, cold, silence and darkness.

The symbols for them are as follows: yang is a single unbroken line; yin is a single broken line.

The structure of the I Ching

The eight trigrams are each made up of three yin and yang lines in various combinations. These are the building blocks of the I Ching and are believed to represent the eight natural forces at work in the universe – Heaven, Earth, Thunder, Water, Mountain, Wind/Wood, Fire and Lake. By creating pairs out of the trigrams, the Chinese created 64 hexagrams (groups of six lines), which represent 64 different states or change, or oracles.

yang

yin

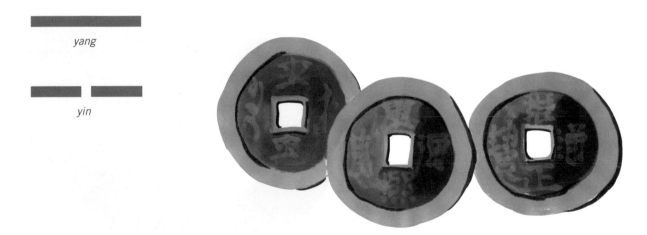

Ancient Chinese coins used for casting the I Ching.

The eight trigrams

These eight fundamental forces in nature can also be used on their own as an oracle. Simply look at the trigrams and decide which you are attracted to, then read the interpretation for the trigram. Or use them to give you deeper insight into the 64 hexagrams on pages 142–157.

Chi'en
The creative

Heaven, sky

Keywords Achievement, Strength, courage, focus
Colour White or gold
This trigram is associated with power, personal motivation and assertiveness. It indicates a desire for personal success and action, and advises it's time to aim high or unleash your potential. Be confident, but don't deny others the right to do their own thing.

K'un
The receptive

Earth

Keyword Acceptance, patience, nourishment, receptivity
Colour Black or brown
Earth represents all that is receptive. It signifies how we take in food, love, how we are nurtured, what makes us feel secure and gives us a sense of belonging. It indicates a need to wait, rather than act, to accept the flow of events. Be grounded but open to change, and things will go according to plan.

Chen
The arousing

Thunder

Keywords Renewal, spontaneity, initiative, surprise
Colour Yellow
The trigram of renewal, like the sudden dramatic thunderstorms in nature which bring rain to create new life. Thunder indicates new beginnings, using your initiative or proving that you are ready to get up and go without question. It can also suggest potency and arousal, awakening to new ideas and sudden flashes of insight.

K'an
The abysmal

Water

Keywords Feeling, emotion, desire, wanting, instinct
Colour Blue
Sometimes we have to let go of reason and rationality, trust our feelings and instincts, not fight them. This trigram indicates that if you go with the flow it may feel risky, but you have no choice. Resist the energy that's working with you and it could work against you.

Ken

Keeping still

Mountain

Keywords Solitude, stillness, silence, withdrawal
Colour Purple
This trigram suggests you need to withdraw from a current situation, to take time to reflect about the issue and not feel you must push for results. It can also indicate that there is a need for stillness in your life, that maybe things are moving too fast, or that you are in need of spiritual awakening.

Sun

The gentle

Wind, wood

Keywords Adaptability, justice, flexibility, fairness
Colour Green
There are times when you must be fair on yourself and not judge your actions or feel guilty for them. This trigram indicates that flexibility and self-awareness are necessary now to resolve any issues. If you can adapt and compromise you will soon be in a position of force rather than weakness.

Li

The clinging

Fire

Keywords Inspiration, communication, clarity, cleansing
Colour Orange
We feel good about ourselves when we're fuelled by the fires of love, desire or success. This trigram indicates action and communication of your dreams and goals. To get on with whatever it is that inspires you. By doing so you will purge yourself of past wounds and have clarity of mind and soul.

Tui

The joyous

Lake

Keywords Secrecy, inner peace, sexual healing, magic
Colour Red
Within you, are all the secrets of the universe, but you do not know it. This trigram indicates getting in touch with your own magic, your sexuality, your psychic insights and your inner guide. Know deep down in your heart that pure pleasure and joy awaits you – it's time to smile at the world.

How to consult the I Ching

To use the coin method of consulting the I Ching, you need to get three coins of the same size, plus some paper and a pen.

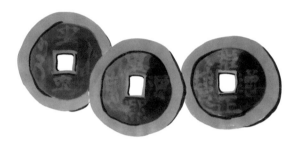

Coin consultation

- Before consulting the oracle, make sure that you have a specific issue or question in your mind that you wish to ask.
- When you feel ready, take your three chosen coins and shake them gently in your cupped hands while you think of your issue or question. Then let them fall gently onto the table or floor and add up their value, as explained below. Each side of the coin represents a value: heads = 3, tails = 2.
- Throw the coins six times. Each throw represents one line of the I Ching hexagram. At the end of each throw, write down the score.

HOW TO INTERPRET YOUR THROWS

- Your first throw represents the first line of the hexagram, starting from the *bottom*.
- Your second throw represents the next line up, and so on.
- A total of 6, 7, 8 or 9 can be obtained in each throw, giving you either a yin (broken) line or a yang (unbroken) line: both 6 and 8 are yin lines; both 7 and 9 are yang lines.

EXAMPLE

Say you threw the following:

- **1st throw:** 2 tails and 1 head = 7
- **2nd throw:** 2 heads and 1 tail = 8
- **3rd throw:** 3 heads = 9
- **4th throw:** 2 tails and 1 head = 7
- **5th throw:** 3 tails = 6
- **6th throw:** 3 tails = 6

You would write down: 789766. And your hexagram would look like this, starting from the bottom and building up:

6 and 8 are yin lines   *7 and 9 are yang lines*

- Now look at the grid opposite. The left-hand column represents your first three throws in ascending order; the top row shows the last three throws in ascending order. In the example given above, your first three throws correspond to the hexagram Li, and your last three throws to the hexagram Chen. The square where they meet gives you the number of the appropriate hexagram. Turn to the relevant page and read its interpretation.

Hexagram grid

	Chi'en	Chen	K'an	Ken	Tui	Li	Sun	K'un
UPPER TRIGRAMS								
Chi'en	1	34	5	26	43	14	9	11
Chen	25	51	3	27	17	21	42	24
K'an	6	40	29	4	47	64	58	7
Ken	33	62	39	52	31	56	53	15
Tui	10	54	60	41	58	38	61	19
Li	13	55	63	22	49	30	37	36
Sun	44	32	48	18	28	50	57	46
K'un	12	16	8	23	45	35	20	2

LOWER TRIGRAMS

Interpreting the hexagrams

Once you have thrown your coins six times and have found the relevant hexagram in the grid on page 141, look up it's meaning in the following pages. Each oracle gives you a keyword to focus on, with a more detailed interpretation for guidance and immediate advice for the future.

1 Chi'en
The creative

Keyword Inspiration
Take control of your life and make a dynamic decision now, so that you can activate your desires and dreams and make them a reality. An encounter with someone older will give you the upper hand in a work or love confrontation. You will get to know a new professional group, where you can be centre-stage or find your true vocation.

2 K'un
The receptive

Keywords Holding back
Listen to advice from those who have experience. Concentrate on developing your personal voice rather than trying to be someone you're not. Be receptive and open to new ideas suggested by female friends or family. If you're looking for love, it is your gentle side that will bring you the romance you yearn.

3 Chun
Difficulties

Keyword Perseverance
Things are chaotic, people don't understand you. Remain calm and accept only genuine advice. There are rivals out there, so go with your instincts about whom you can trust. Progress will be made if you don't force the issue. Keep your head down and the energy will soon be less chaotic.

4 Meng
Immaturity

Keyword Inexperience
Your enthusiasm is great, but don't get too carried away with impossible dreams. You have a childlike charm, but remember that a beginner's luck eventually runs out. You must listen to people who have experience if you are to succeed in your goals. If you have a relationship issue, you are about to leap into the deep end without truly knowing what you want.

5 Hsu
Waiting

Keyword Patience
A current problem is going to be resolved, although perhaps not in the way you had hoped for. Remain calm and confident, and accept that things are as they should be. Self-discipline will be needed to solve a relationship dilemma. Outside influences require careful handling.

6 Sung
Conflict

Keyword Communication
To avoid conflict, you must speak up and let someone know how you truly feel. Confrontation only generates more challenge, so don't rise to the bait. People will confront your views whether you like it or not. Stay calm and everyone will benefit from your balanced outlook. Defuse an emotional clash of wills before it gets messy.

7 Shih
The army

Keyword Support
It feels as if everyone is rebelling and your gut feeling is to do your own thing, too. But success or happiness will be achieved only if you can provide leadership and support in your family, workplace or love relationships. Be an inspiration rather than a damp squib. It is your chance to show that you can take responsibility for your actions.

8 Pi
Holding together

Keyword Harmony
Be yourself. Express your feelings and try not to seek approval for everything you do. Be wary of certain people who could lead you astray from your personal direction. In a love issue, don't try to cling to someone because they want more space. Have your own freedom, too. Be really truthful about your feelings and the future will be true to you.

9 Hsaio ch'u
Taming by the small

Keyword Humility
Plant the seeds now for future success. What you do today will reap rewards tomorrow. Don't let self-doubt or fear of the unknown put you off-course. Be prepared to adapt to someone else's ideas rather than thinking you know all the answers. Be humble rather than proud, and love will come to you.

10 Lu
Conduct

Keyword Simplicity
In a relationship question this hexagram reveals that you must be good-humoured and honest about your desires. If you keep an open mind, you will be able to walk on dangerous territory with a degree of safety. Someone will soon accept you for who you are, rather than try to change you.

11 Tai
Peace

Keyword Prosperity
This is a great time for new beginnings. Anything you start now will be to your benefit in the months to come. But don't get complacent just because things are looking up. The feel-good factor may be coming your way, but remember that happiness is rooted in your behaviour. Don't boast about your success or manipulate anyone, as this could lead to your ultimate downfall.

12 P'i
Standstill

Keyword Blockage
Instead of positive growth, you feel blocked by circumstances beyond your control. But being in limbo also gives you time to reflect on your actions and future desires. Withdraw from silly confrontations and wait for better times. This hexagram can also signify that someone will try to prevent you from moving on or changing your lifestyle.

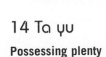

13 T'ung jen
Fellowship

Keyword Cooperation
There must be no hidden agendas between you and others. If you want to succeed in your plans, honesty is essential. Cooperate with work colleagues to ensure the success of a business venture. Talk things through with a lover and respect each other's space and freedom. This hexagram also indicates that compromise will bring good results.

14 Ta yu
Possessing plenty

Keyword Abundance
You are about to enter a great phase of abundance, whether in love, materialism or personal success. There will be envious people out there, so take care not to become arrogant about what you have. If you abuse your strength, you will lose it. Be a guiding light for others, rather than shining your own light directly in their faces. Don't become possessive of a lover or you could lose them.

15 Ch'ien
Modesty

Keywords Quiet progress
If you maintain an air of serenity in all your dealings, you will make progress towards any love or professional goal. But it won't happen overnight. Be prepared for others to be aggressive or pretentious, but remain calmly assertive yourself. This is not the time to be conceited. Keep cool and calm and you will receive the respect you deserve.

16 Yu
Enthusiasm

Keyword Energy
You will soon be given an opportunity to prove that you are irrepressible. Any new ideas can be communicated and your enthusiasm and initiative will be taken into account by others. Just make sure that your motivation stems from a real awareness of what is right and what is wrong.

17 Su
Following

Keyword Acceptance
It's time to accept your limitations and those of others. If you are asking a relationship question, you will soon be able to welcome change rather than fear it. It's time to say goodbye to those people or ideas that conflict with your true values. Honour your own; don't live by others' expectations of you.

18 Ku
Removing corruption

Keyword Renovation
Make it clear what you will and won't do. It's time to redress the balance, show your strength of character, make decisions that are rooted in your individual beliefs. Renovate your psychological make-up as you would a house. Your efforts at self-repair will be noticed by someone who can open the doors to a new career or love affair.

19 Lin
Approach

Keyword Advance
Success and progress are coming to you now. But the way you approach life is equally important for the future. You must look at the world with a wider perspective. Accept new challenges, help others, enjoy unexpected opportunities and never give up on simply being yourself.

20 Kuan
Contemplation

Keyword Reflection
You have greater knowledge than you thought, so don't deny your right to speak up and tell someone your beliefs or opinions. Just don't try to force-feed them with your ideas, or it could all backfire on you. In the next few weeks it would be wise to reflect carefully on any decision rather than leap in at the deep end.

21 Shih ho
Biting through

Keyword Obstacle
The same old problem seems to keep getting in the way of progress. Now is your chance to 'bite through' the apparent problem by being frank about what you truly want. In the very near future you will have to deal with others who are difficult and obstinate, but with objectivity you can persuade them to your way of thinking.

22 Pi
Grace

Keyword Beauty
Be sincere, and let your true beauty shine through. Remember that the external appearance of happiness is often false and success isn't always about material wealth. Believe in your inner voice and in the months to come, others will see you in a new light. You will have the grace and charm to attract anyone to you.

23 Po
Splitting apart

Keyword Non-action
Everything in your life seems to be falling apart: relationships are fraught, work is stormy. But in the weeks to come, your strength of purpose and patience will bring you the harmony you seek. Resist the urge to provoke others or interfere. This situation won't last long if you accept that things are as they must be.

24 Fu
Return

Keywords Turning point
You are on the threshold of an exciting period of good fortune. Don't fear change – make it your friend, drop bad habits, dump outmoded ideas and welcome the new and different. Things will progress as you want them to, as long as you are conscious of your actions and make decisions accordingly.

25 Wu wang
Innocence

Keyword Intuition
Live for the moment, rather than dwelling on past mistakes or regretting what you have done. The future will unfold in the way you want, if you trust your intuition and don't worry about what will be. Any problem will quickly disappear when you encounter someone who offers good advice.

26 Ta ch'u
Taming by the great

Keyword Calm
Remain calm. Don't let your feelings take over your rational nature. If you are caught up in a difficult decision or situation right now, stay cool and it will soon be resolved. A down-to-earth friend or admirer will bring you the news you've been waiting for.

27 I
The open mouth

Keyword Discipline
Nurture your gentle side. Don't become arrogant or too proud to listen to others. Friends and lovers are there to support you, but don't demand too much from them in return. In the future you won't have to make any more personal sacrifices. Self-discipline and motivation – not wishful thinking – will bring you success.

28 Ta kuo
Preponderance of the great

Keyword Pressure
This hexagram indicates that you're going through a period of great struggle or pressure. You feel tempted, understandably, to run away from the issue. But you can't escape yourself, so hold back and think things through. To progress, the problem must be resolved. You may have to make a small sacrifice now to get things right for the future.

29 K'an
The abysmal

Keywords Emotional depths
You know what is right for you, so don't ignore your heart. Go with the flow of your own nature. Denying your feelings will only cause more heartache. Embrace change rather than struggle against it. Emotional honesty is needed in the future to ensure that you make the right decision. Be open, receptive and, above all, be alert to your own weaknesses.

30 Li
The clinging

Keyword Passion
You are clinging to someone or something too tightly, as if your life depends on it. And that passion is preventing you from living out your true potential. Realize that you have your own autonomy. With an inner passion for life and love, stand up for your own principles and don't fear being yourself. Someone will adore you for the inner spark that is about to be lit.

31 Hsien
Influence

Keyword Union
This hexagram signifies that an outside influence is coming into your life and you will have to liaise or involve yourself more deeply with that person, idea or set of circumstances. It also indicates courtship, mutual happiness, a love affair or even marriage.

32 Heng
Duration

Keyword Stamina
Expecting too much too soon will only lead to disappointment. But you have the strength and determination to wait for things to change, even though it feels as if you must act now or never. Don't compare yourself to others or try to be someone you're not. Good fortune will come from integrity and self-belief.

33 Tun
Retreat

Keyword Withdrawal
However hard it is to retreat from a negative situation, this hexagram indicates that you must do so and not see that retreat as a failure. It's timely to withdraw, so take a long, hard look at the issues involved and prepare yourself for a more favourable time when you can get going with your plans.

34 Ta chuang
Power of the great

Keyword Empowerment
In a professional or relationship problem, you know that you could force things to a head, but make sure you're not trying to control and manipulate someone or play power games. Real self-empowerment comes from emotional honesty. Someone could be about to power-trip you, so be aware of overt charmers or false praise.

35 Chin
Progress

Keyword Sunrise
This hexagram signifies great progress. Whatever you want to achieve can be realized, as long as you remember that your judgement could become cloudy if you are too self-centred. In a relationship issue, someone will soon see your inner beauty shining through. But don't give up your freedom for the sake of approval.

36 Ming I
Darkening of the light

Keyword Sunset
Realize that you are on the wrong track, that it's time to re-evaluate your plans and leave the situation now while you can. It would be foolish to persevere with something that will bring you only confusion. It may take time to get things off the ground, but when there's a sunset you can be sure that there's always another sunrise.

37 Chia jen
The family

Keyword Loyalty
A harmonious relationship is indicated here, as long as you clarify your emotional boundaries. Ironically, if you both know your limitations, you can both act more freely. Happiness will come to you if you accept that loyalty works both ways, so don't try to live by double standards.

38 K'uei
Opposition

Keyword Misunderstanding
Life seems threatening, and people don't understand you. Nothing seems fair, but it's only because you're projecting all your fears, worries, hates and hurts onto the external world. From now on, if you give out goodness, allow someone closer to your heart and trust in the universe; life will be on your side, not seemingly against you.

39 Chien
Obstruction

Keyword Deadlock
A friend or lover won't make an effort, and you are so wrapped up in your personal problems that you haven't got the time of day to motivate him or her. Your lack of body language suggests that you're both stuck in personal mud, unable to free yourselves from the deadlock. Don't blame yourself or anyone else for the situation. In a few days all will be resolved.

40 Hsieh
Deliverance

Keyword Release
It's time to forgive and forget – don't brood on past hurts or feelings of rejection. Now is the time to move on, dump your emotional baggage and live for the present. Free yourself from old illusions and you will soon be in a position to overcome any obstacles. Don't hang out with people who don't understand that you have a quest to fulfil.

41 Sun
Decrease

Keyword Restriction
You are now entering
a phase of limitation.
Don't underestimate
your talents or goals,
but take the softly, softly
approach when dealing
with others. The more
laid-back and sincere
you are, the more likely
you are to succeed.
Rushing ahead will
simply weaken your
argument or impede
your progress.

42 I
Increase

Keyword Gain
Be creative with your
ideas and you will win
the praise you're seeking.
Someone will soon be
willing to give you a
chance to improve your
status or income. Be
generous and kind, and
you will receive the good
things of life. Don't
assume things will just
fall into your lap – you
need to work for your
goals, too.

43 Kuai
Breakthrough

Keyword Success
You have reached a
turning point where you
know that over the
horizon good times are
coming. Self-confidence
and focus are essential
if you are to continue
making headway. Don't
be provoked into doing
something you don't feel
is right for you – it's time
to stand up for your
rights and opinions.

44 Kou
Coming to meet

Keyword Temptation
You just can't resist
someone or something
that is not good for you.
And however hard you
try, you can't rid yourself
of the desire. You have
no choice but to follow
your instincts, but don't
get too involved or you
will lose touch with your
better judgement. Trust
your suspicions, for they
are usually right.

45 Ts'ui
Gathering together

Keyword Leadership
Get together with like-minded people whom you know you can trust and you will soon be rewarded for your spirit and enterprise. Remain focused on your goals, but don't try to go it alone right now. Make sure that you are working for the good of everyone involved and not just for your benefit.

46 Sheng
Pushing upwards

Keyword Growth
This hexagram indicates that you can now achieve whatever you set out to do, as long as you don't get led astray by those who want to manipulate you. How a goal is achieved is often more important than the goal itself. Welcome new opportunities that will give you the chance to progress quickly.

47 K'un
Oppression

Keyword Worry
You feel as if you have no energy, that the world is a harsh place and no one is listening. These are testing times, and there seems to be no way out of a difficult situation. Resist the feelings of gloom and look within for inner strength. In a few weeks you will wonder why you ever felt down, when a surprise encounter suddenly lifts you to a real high.

48 Ching
The well

Keyword Wisdom
This hexagram signifies that it's time to unleash your talents. You have greater depths of wisdom than you give yourself credit for, so rather than avoid your inner truth, discover it, nurture it and become wise yourself. If you are asking a relationship question, then a wiser, older lover or partner will change your life for the better.

49 Ko
Revolution

Keyword Change
Consider what motivates
you right now, and
whether you really want
to change something in
your life. If so, then it's
time to act. Preparation
is all. Radical change
is inevitable, but be
responsible for the
change rather than
waiting for it to come
to you. Make sure you
know what it is in your
life that needs to be
revolutionized and why.

50 Ting
The cauldron

Keyword Nourishment
You can be assured of
success as long as you
are honest and open.
Someone will be envious
of your achievement,
so watch out for those
who begrudge you your
happiness. Avoid feeling
guilty because you've
more status or self-
confidence than someone
else. Nurture your
dreams and you will
make them real.

51 Chen
The arousing

Keyword Shock
This hexagram represents
unforeseen and unpred-
ictable events. Are you
currently in shock, or are
you shocking others?
Likewise, do unexpected
or major events unnerve
you, or are you excited
by the buzz? If you are
'shocked', accept that
the shock will bring you
fresh insights soon, and
represents a turning
point in altering
something that is 'not
right' in your life. If you
are unshockable or
shocking yourself, it's
time to make a fresh
start and get out of a rut.

52 Ken
Keeping still

Keyword Stillness
Be calm, detached and
objective about your
current issue or question.
If you keep calm, things
will work out the way you
want them to. Don't let
other people distract you,
and in a few days you
will see the answer to a
problem with clarity.

53 Chien
Development

Keywords Step by step
Even though you know
where you are going,
don't rush into things or
you might regret it later.
Don't have such high
expectations that no one
– not even yourself – can
live up to them. In a
relationship it will take
time for a commitment
to be made or a change
of heart to be revealed.

54 Kuei mei
Marrying maiden

Keyword Desire
Someone may let you
down or not be as
interested in you as you
are in them. It's time to
honour your individuality,
rather than assume that
someone else provides
the key to your
happiness. If you are
looking for romance, this
hexagram indicates that
an admirer is already out
there. Look where you
least expect to.

55 Feng
Abundance

Keyword Plenty
Trust in your instincts:
right now your influence
is powerful and you can
achieve great things.
But don't get arrogant,
because you will only be
alienated by those you
want to be with. Live for
the present, forget the
past and move on while
you have the chance.

56 Lu
The wanderer

Keyword Travel
Although you feel content
with the way things are,
you're not really satisfied.
You know you must move
on from a relationship or
a specific lifestyle. It's
time to travel, either
literally visiting foreign
shores or simply
progressing on your own
life journey. Do so in
style, but – as with any
unfamiliar territory –
respect the new and your
journey will be a joy.

57 Sun
The gentle

Keyword Consistency
Being gentle doesn't mean you have to be soft. Be firm about your intentions to someone and don't let them manipulate you. If you are consistently honest about your beliefs and goals, they will happen. Things may not have gone the way you hoped, but with persistence you will reap great rewards.

58 Tui
The joyous

Keyword Fulfilment
You want more, but material gain doesn't make life better; it just creates a vicious circle. For lasting happiness you must look to yourself. What are your needs and objectives? Are you honouring them? Very soon an encounter with someone will create real joy and give you the freedom to be yourself.

59 Huan
Dispersion

Keyword Rigidity
If you are fixed and stubborn, you won't be able to create the openings you need for success. It would be appropriate now to sacrifice a short-term goal for a long-term benefit. Alternatively, a loved one is finding it hard to see things any way other than their own. Dissolve the emotional ice with understanding and humour.

60 Chieh
Limitation

Keyword Moderation
Know your own limitations, and do everything in moderation now. Start saying 'No' when you mean it, rather than 'Yes' just to keep the peace or gain approval. If someone won't take no for an answer, ask them which part of the word they don't understand.

61 Chung fu
Inner truth

Keyword Acceptance
This hexagram indicates that you're now growing more independent than certain people would like. You have a right to do your own thing, as long as it is generated by inner truth. If you are trying to persuade someone of the right way to act, lead by example and they will soon follow in your footsteps.

62 Hsiao kuo
Preponderance of the small

Keyword Non-action
Although you want to seek solutions or do something to right a situation, it will only make matters worse. Bide your time, wait for the air to clear and don't take risks. Seek help from someone older and wiser, who can give you objective advice. In the weeks to come you will make progress, however difficult it seems now.

63 Chi chi
After completion

Keyword Order
This hexagram signifies balance, harmony and order. The scales aren't tipped in anyone's favour, and awareness, clarity and insight are coming your way. But be wary of thinking glibly that all will be well for ever. Out of chaos comes order, but this can change in an instant if you are not prepared to work at a relationship problem.

64 Wei chi
Before completion

Keyword Dedication
You want to take control of your life and feel a real sense of vocation. But to do so you must dedicate yourself to your talents, skills and self-development. Times are changing and very soon, someone will see your true potential. Make sure you are ready, prepared and clear about what you really want.

CRYSTAL ZODIAC

8 • CRYSTAL ZODIAC

By choosing your own crystals they become your personal guides and talismans, offering divinatory and protective power simultaneously. You can buy ready-made sets of crystals, but the more personal your choice, the more they will energize the direction you are seeking.

What can crystals reveal about your future?

Crystals have been used for fortune-telling throughout history for their subtle vibrational nature, which is thought to be linked to the vibrational powers of the cosmos. They open the gateway to deeper knowledge and your own inner wisdom and intuition. As a divinatory tool, they can be cast onto a zodiac circle, to harness the power of the planetary forces and protect against negative energies. Or they can be laid out in a spread, like Tarot cards and runes. Alternatively, you can pick one from a pouch or bag, as your guide crystal for the day. You can also align your own energy to your personal zodiac crystal vibration and benefit from its miraculous properties by wearing the crystal all day long.

The benefits of using crystals
- Identify influences and energies in your life.
- Learn what challenges you need to overcome.
- Know what sort of day you can expect.
- Discover instant solutions to questions.
- Find out your guiding crystal for future happiness.
- Discover what the future holds.

Uncannily, you will find that events and encounters through the day align with the symbolism of that crystal, or empower you with it's specific qualities. For example, say you randomly chose aquamarine, the chances are that you will have a flirtatious or romantic encounter!

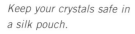

Keep your crystals safe in a silk pouch.

The history of the crystal zodiac

As long ago as 4000 BCE the Chaldaean people of Mesopotamia used astrology and the stars to predict the future. They also believed that crystals found in the earth were linked to planets, which reflect the vibrations of the cosmos. From the earliest times crystals have been regarded as possessing divinatory powers: the ancient Greeks believed that every piece of clear quartz crystal is a fragment of the archetypal Crystal of Truth. Each of the 12 signs of the zodiac also corresponds to a crystal and, in turn each crystal aligns with the energies associated with that astrological sign.

Choosing crystals for divination

For the crystal zodiac in this book, you ideally need each of the crystals described overleaf (see pages 162–163), but if you can't get hold of them all, you can replace some with other crystals associated with the zodiac signs (which you can easily find out in any New Age shop).

Buy flat, oval-shaped crystals, and hold each crystal in your hand until you 'know intuitively' it's the one that is right for you. It might feel very cold or very hot, or almost as if it's vibrating in your palm. If you get a reaction – especially an intuitive 'flash' – then you're in tune with the vibrational energy of the crystal and therefore with the cosmos.

Clear quartz crystal vibrates clarily, which will help you to see the way forward out of any difficult situation.

Your planetary crystals

Each planet in the solar system rules a zodiac sign (apart from Venus and Mercury which rule two signs each) and corresponds to specific energies of the associated crystals. Look up the interpretations below when you cast or draw these stones.

The Sun rules Leo

Clear quartz crystal

Like the Sun, clear quartz crystal represents direct, potent energy. It is the crystal of action, focus and potential. When you draw clear quartz in a reading you know it's time to act from the heart, to get on with your goals, fulfil those dreams and enjoy being yourself. Wear or carry this crystal if you need to start afresh.

The Moon rules Cancer

Opal

The moon represents intuitive, feeling energy and, similarly the opal, embodies a moody, translucent aura. When you draw your Moon crystal in a reading, it reminds you to respect your intuition and your emotions. Wear or carry opal to feel more in tune with others or to develop your sixth sense.

Mercury rules Gemini and Virgo

Topaz

Mercury is the planet of 'magical communication', and when you draw topaz, it indicates that you must now communicate your desires, open your mind to other ideas and express yourself clearly. Wear or carry your Mercury crystal to aid decision-making or for happy travelling.

Venus rules Taurus and Libra

Tourmaline

Venus represents beauty, love and affairs of the heart. When you draw or cast your Venus crystal, new relationships are favoured and romance or deeper love will develop. It's time to use your heart not your head. Wear or carry tourmaline to promote harmony and tolerance.

Mars rules Aries

Red agate

Mars is the planet of confidence and desire. And red agate represents this fiery spirit of potent leadership. When you draw or cast red agate, you are ready to defend your rights or those of others. You may feel frustrated by events, but now's the time to initiate what is right for you. Wear or carry red agate when you need a shot of courage.

Jupiter rules Sagittarius

Lapis lazuli

This stone has always been known as the 'eye of wisdom' and, like Jupiter, represents truth and meaning in life. When you draw lapis, career matters, wider knowledge and ideals are important to you now. Carry this stone when you want to discover deeper truths.

The ten planetary crystals

Planet		Crystal	Keyword	Active / Passive
Sun		Clear quartz crystal	Clarity	Active
Moon		Opal	Sensitivity	Passive
Mercury		Topaz	Understanding	Active
Venus		Tourmaline	Compassion	Passive
Mars		Red agate	Progress	Active
Jupiter		Lapis lazuli	Wisdom	Passive
Saturn		Onyx	Structure	Passive
Uranus		Orange carnelian	Rebellion	Active
Neptune		Blue lace agate	Vision	Active
Pluto		Amethyst	Passion	Active

Saturn rules Capricorn

Onyx

Saturn represents order and definition. When you draw or cast onyx, limitations may be holding you up, but the reality is that your determination will see you through any delays. Realize that it's time to define who you are and your true values. Carry onyx when you want to achieve your goals.

Uranus rules Aquarius

Orange carnelian

This stone was worn to protect against envy and, like Uranus, it represents freedom from the expectations of others. It's time to make progress and however way-out your thinking, it's through change and rebellion against the status quo that you will become true to yourself. Wear your Uranian crystal when you need to break free.

Neptune rules Pisces

Blue lace agate

When you draw your Neptune crystal, it's time to relinquish worn-out ideas and habits and instigate a new vision for your future. Accept that wherever you go you can't escape yourself. Carry blue lace agate if you feel confused and need clarity, or to promote self-awareness.

Pluto rules Scorpio

Amethyst

Pluto represents our bottom-line survival instinct, our passion for life. Likewise, when worn or carried, amethyst absorbs negativity and allows you to be fearless in the face of change. When you draw the Pluto stone, accept that you have come to the end of one cycle of your life and must now move on to the next with passion and self-belief.

Your zodiac crystals

The crystals below correspond to each sign of the zodiac and along with the ten planetary crystals, they make up a complete set of 22. Don't worry if you can't get hold of them all. Start with ten that you really like, but make sure there is a good range of colour and meaning.

Choosing and using crystals

Check the keyword qualities beside each crystal to ensure that you haven't chosen ten crystals that are all active, with no passive ones. Depending on which sign of the zodiac you are, always carry, wear or keep in a safe place your own zodiac crystal. This will give you confidence, self-belief, vitality and the ability to express your true potential and chosen pathway.

Check the keywords and phrases on the zodiac wheel relating to your sun-sign. If they sound unfamiliar, place the crystal under your pillow to enhance those qualities that you might be lacking in.

The 12 zodiac crystals

Zodiac sign		Crystal	Keyword	Active / Passive
♈	Aries	Red carnelian	Activate	Active
♉	Taurus	Rose quartz	Love	Passive
♊	Gemini	Citrine	Communicate	Active
♋	Cancer	Moonstone	Embrace	Passive
♌	Leo	Tiger's eye	Inspire	Active
♍	Virgo	Peridot	Discriminate	Passive
♎	Libra	Jade	Harmonize	Passive
♏	Scorpio	Malachite	Transform	Active
♐	Sagittarius	Turquoise	Travel	Active
♑	Capricorn	Obsidian	Materialize	Active
♒	Aquarius	Amber	Rationalize	Passive
♓	Pisces	Aquamarine	Romance	Passive

Zodiac wheel

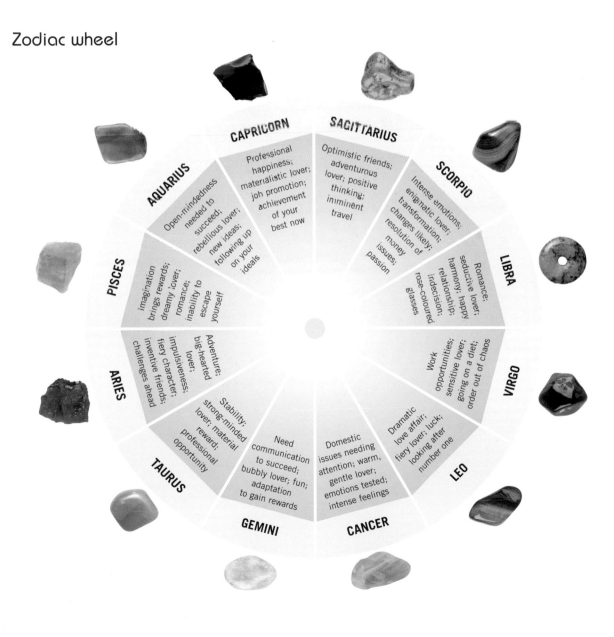

CAPRICORN — Professional happiness; materialistic lover; job promotion; achievement of your best now

SAGITTARIUS — Optimistic friends; adventurous lover; positive thinking; imminent travel

SCORPIO — Intense emotions; enigmatic lover; transformation; changes likely; resolution of money issues; passion

AQUARIUS — Open-mindedness needed to succeed; rebellious lover; new ideas; following up on your ideals

LIBRA — Romance; seductive lover; harmony; happy relationship; indecision; rose-coloured glasses

PISCES — Imagination brings rewards; dreamy lover; romance; inability to escape yourself

VIRGO — Work opportunities; sensitive lover; going on a diet; order out of chaos

ARIES — Adventure; big-hearted lover; impulsiveness; fiery character; inventive friends; challenges ahead

LEO — Dramatic love affair; fiery lover; luck; looking after number one

TAURUS — Stability; strong-minded lover; material reward; professional opportunity

GEMINI — Need communication to succeed; bubbly lover; fun; adaptation to gain rewards

CANCER — Domestic issues needing attention; warm, gentle lover; emotions tested; intense feelings

Casting crystals onto a zodiac circle

This divinatory method is fun to do. You can either copy the zodiac circle on page 165 onto a large piece of paper or cloth or mark out the circle with thread.

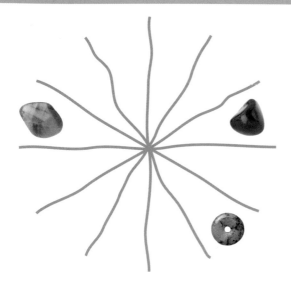

Create your own zodiac circle with threads or stones.

- Place your crystals in a drawstring pouch or bag.
- Sit or kneel in front of your circle and focus on your particular question. For example, you might want to ask, 'When can I expect new love to come into my life?'
- Pick a single crystal from the bag, without looking, then cast it onto the circle.
- Whichever zodiac sign it lands on, check the zodiac circle for keywords to help your interpretation.
- Then draw and cast a second and third crystal.

HOW TO INTERPRET YOUR CASTING
- The first crystal you cast is the Crystal of Light. It represents your current situation. It doesn't matter which crystal you throw – it is where it falls in the circle that matters. Say the crystal lands in the slice of the circle devoted to Libra. Turn to the zodiac wheel on page 165 to check which qualities Libra signifies. As your question concerned love, this indicates that romance and harmony are favoured right now. The closer the crystal lands to the middle of the circle, the sooner events will unfurl; the nearer the outer edge of the circle, the longer it will take. I usually work on the principle that if it's about halfway between the centre and the edge, this is equivalent to one week; on the edge of the circle is nearer two weeks. If the crystal falls outside the circle, then the time is not yet right for the necessary change or request to take place.
- The second crystal you cast is the Crystal of Shadows. This represents the people, or outside influences and blockages, which could affect your desires and dreams and which you have to deal with right now. Say the crystal lands on Leo. This indicates that a fiery, progressive friend will be the key to your romantic encounter, but this could indicate a rival – so watch out!
- The last crystal you throw is the Crystal of Fortune. This indicates the outcome of your question. Say the crystal lands on Gemini, near the edge of the circle. This means that good communication and a light-hearted approach to life will create the romantic dream you're looking for, but you might have to wait for a couple more weeks.

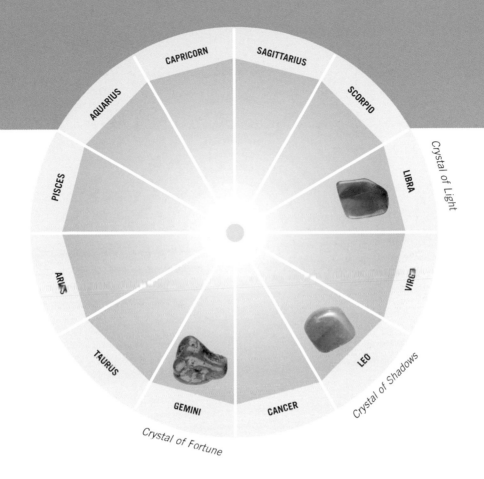

CAPRICORN

SAGITTARIUS

AQUARIUS

SCORPIO

PISCES

LIBRA

Crystal of Light

ARIES

VIRGO

TAURUS

LEO

Crystal of Shadows

GEMINI

CANCER

Crystal of Fortune

Crystals cast onto a zodiac circle

Choose a crystal for the day

You can also choose a single crystal to find out what sort of day you are going to have.

- Gently shake your crystals in their pouch or bag and then take one crystal out and place it in the centre of a cloth.
- Study it, feel what it means to you and look up its interpretation on pages 168–171.
- Next, take the crystal in your hands, close your eyes and attune yourself to the crystal vibrations. Let its energy flow through your hands and throughout your body; invite the good qualities of the crystal into your world to empower you.

- Return the crystal to the bag, or keep it in your pocket or a safe place throughout the day to energize you with its specific qualities. Depending on the meaning of the crystal in question, you will know what kind of day you can expect and how to act and express the energy in a positive, life-enhancing way. For example, if you chose red agate, you would need to express your feelings honestly or vividly.

Crystal oracles

Here are simple but varied interpretations of the 22 crystals used in this book. Always widen your interpretation to relate to the question or issue at stake; develop your intuition and work with the vibrational energy of the crystal to help you reach a more detailed analysis.

Red carnelian

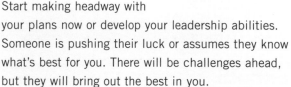

Keyword Activate
You are driven to succeed. It's time to conquer your fears or self-doubt about what you can achieve. Start making headway with your plans now or develop your leadership abilities. Someone is pushing their luck or assumes they know what's best for you. There will be challenges ahead, but they will bring out the best in you.

Rose quartz

Keyword Love
A love match is well favoured or a great rapport will develop between you and someone new. You are about to fall in love – just make sure that it's not an illusion. Sensual pleasure is more important to you than ambition and it's timely to take a break or relax with friends. All aspects of relationships can be sorted out now.

Citrine

Keyword Communicate
Communicate with someone to whom you've never spoken to before and you will learn something valuable. Focus on your goals and you will fulfil your ambitions. Citrine enables you to transform negative thoughts into positive action. You can also make a good decision now, based on logic and objectivity. Travel is favoured and can bring you happiness.

Moonstone

Keyword Embrace
Trust in your intuition and connect to your inner wisdom. Your moods and feelings may be confused, so try to take a more objective look at the issue involved. Take care that you aren't being deceived by those who want to have some power over you. Be aware of wider family values, but make sure that you honour your own. Are they different?

Tiger's eye

Keyword Inspire
You are ready to go on a quest or to inspire others with your talents. Develop your potential and don't let others tell you what you should or shouldn't do with your life. Now is the time to dare to be different, and show that you have purpose and vision. Love relationships will be dramatic and challenging.

Peridot

Keyword Discriminate
Make decisions based on facts, not on feelings. You need meaningful relationships, not superficial friends. It's time to spread your wings, or interact with people who can respect your individuality. Discriminate with care, because you will have to make a very important choice in the future.

Jade

Keyword Harmonize
Love and harmony are well indicated, and you will have success in romance. However, don't get wrapped up in sentimentality or become a victim of emotional blackmail. You're in harmony with the universe, so ask for what you truly want.

Malachite

Keyword Transform
Known as the 'sleep stone' because of its apparently hypnotic affect, this stone indicates that you can transform your life as long as you stay awake to

opportunity. You're at last sailing out of choppy emotional waters into calmer ones. If the issue concerns money or material affairs, you will soon have much success.

Turquoise

Keyword Travel
Journeys are indicated, both physical and intellectual ones. Explore your motives: are they your own, or has someone forced you to act the way you do? Expand your repertoire of talents and qualities. Watch out for someone who promises the world and can't follow through. Love is boundless.

Obsidian

Keyword Materialize
Persevere in your ambitions; don't give in to criticism or self-doubt. There will be challenging influences or setbacks to a plan, but these will in turn instigate a wonderful run of events. Welcome any changes, for they will ultimately bring positive results. You can now ground a goal or aim, and prove your worth.

Amber

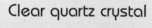

Keyword Rationalize
You are rebellious and
visionary, and the time
is right to make those
radical changes that you
know are inevitable. Rationalizing a situation, rather
than dwelling on the rights and wrongs involved, will
resolve the issue.

Opal

Keyword Sensitivity
Feelings are running
high. Be sensitive to your
long-term goals and
nurture them. You can't
change things that cannot be changed. Accept that
someone cannot be anything other than who they are.

Aquamarine

Keyword Romance
Harmonious feelings and
romance are in the air.
The tide is turning in
your favour. Don't let
other people's negative emotions get you down, and
don't compromise for the sake of peace.

Topaz

Keyword Understanding
You need to be more open
and less judgemental in
your relationships.
Understanding and
tolerance will bring you
the results you're aiming for. Someone is making
you feel invisible – don't let them.

Clear quartz crystal

Keyword Clarity
You can see clearly the
way forward out of any
difficult situation. You
will soon be filled with
enthusiasm, joy and a sense of personal success.
Happiness is within sight, if you believe in yourself.

Tourmaline

Keyword Compassion
With true friends and
compassion for others
you will feel rich in
spirit. You will find true
love, if you respect your
own needs. A lover is now ready to commit.

Red agate

Keyword Progress
You are justifiably angry and it's time to express your feelings – don't bottle them up. Progress will be made if you take courage and crusade for your rights. A stranger brings unexpected welcome rewards.

Orange carnelian

Keyword Rebellion
Innovative change will promote positive life choices. Others are frustrating you because they don't agree with your viewpoint, but press ahead with your plans. A partner or lover won't make a commitment.

Lapis lazuli

Keyword Wisdom
Use your head and not your heart. Talk to people who have good advice to offer you or who are very experienced. You can now forge ahead with all career matters.

Blue lace agate

Keyword Vision
Worldly success can be yours, if you give as much as you take. You have extraordinary imagination, so make use of it. Your vision of the future is great – don't sacrifice it on behalf of others.

Amethyst

Keyword Passion
A passionate love affair is indicated. It's time to close one door and open another. There will be a powerful shift in consciousness or lifestyle transformation for the better. Extremes of feeling mean that someone (maybe it's you?) can't decide whether to go or stay, love or hate, give in or resist.

Onyx

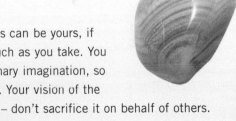

Keyword Structure
You are now in control of your life, so make sure it is what you want it to be. Structure and organization are needed or you will be in chaos. Material wealth matters to someone more than love.

Crystal spreads

You can also use the crystals as spreads to ask specific questions, to find out whether you are compatible with someone, for example, and which issues you need to resolve in your life for future happiness.

Preparation

Ideally, use a special cloth or silk scarf on a table for these readings. Alternatively, the most natural place to read crystals is out in the open: near the sea, on a beach or in a garden. The crystals are particularly powerful around the crescent and full-moon cycles and at specific times of the year, such as the spring and summer equinox and the summer and winter solstices.

Always prepare by using a meditation technique, burning incense or lighting candles; or, if you are outside, cast an imaginary magical circle around you by pointing with your finger in a huge circle as you turn 360 degrees. First, cast the circle clockwise, then anti-clockwise – this will protect you and your crystals and will vitalize your own energy to resonate with the cosmos.

Destiny spread

This simple spread enables you to find out which issues need to be resolved for your future happiness.
• Pick a total of five crystals from your pouch, and lay them out in the order shown below left.

1 Your current mood
2 Your future desire
3 What you really want
4 The issue that needs resolving
5 Direction/outcome

HOW TO INTERPRET THE SPREAD
• Each crystal represents a different aspect of your own destiny.

EXAMPLE
1 Your current mood – turquoise: You're restless and have itchy feet.
2 Your future desire – malachite: You're dreaming of material success.
3 What you really want – amethyst: Deep down you want more passion in your life.
4 The issue that needs resolving – red carnelian: You need to sort out whether your aspirations are really your own.
5 Direction/outcome – clear quartz crystal: You will soon have clarity about your true goals.

Compatibility spread

This spread is useful when you want to know if someone's energy is compatible with your own.

Do you have an affinity with a new friend? Can you trust a rebellious colleague? Is a new lover going to be a perfect match?

• Pick one crystal at a time from your pouch, until you have chosen five, and lay them out in the order shown below.

1 Me now
2 The other now
3 Together now
4 Your test
5 Your destiny together

HOW TO INTERPRET THE SPREAD

• Each crystal represents a different element of the relationship in question.

EXAMPLE: **You've recently been promoted at work, but a once-friendly colleague seems to dislike you – can you be friends again?**

1 Me now – blue lace agate: You feel as if you've sacrificed a friendship for your goals. There are too many undercurrents of feeling and you can't work happily.

2 The other now – tourmaline: Your colleague is a compassionate, warm-hearted person, but dare not reveal that she's envious of your success.

3 Together now – red agate: If you get together now, the chances are you will have a big row, expressing all your anger at each other and then getting on with work again, but she'll still be seething. It won't necessarily resolve the issue.

4 Your test – lapis lazuli: Your test is to widen your social network, make new friends and work contacts, and laugh. Be the progressive person you are and place value on those who admire you for your skills.

5 Your destiny together – amber: She will soon be objective enough to realize that her behaviour is childish and you will become friends again.

Index

Acknowledgements

Executive Editor Sandra Rigby
Editor Jessica Cowie
Executive Art Editor Sally Bond
Designer Patrick McLeavey
Illustrator KJA-artists.com
Picture Researcher Sophie Delpech
Production Controller Simone Nauerth

Picture Acknowledgements

AKG, London 6, 60. **Corbis UK Ltd** 61; /Austrian Archives 61; /Tracy Kahn 7 top right; /Craig Lovell 4 top right, 109; /Marko Modic 136. **Getty Images**/ Richard Ashworth 4 centre right, 82. **ImageSource** 119 top left, 119 top right. **Octopus Publishing Group Limited** 51, 53, 56, 113, 120 top centre, 120 top left, 121 top centre, 121 top left, 121 top right; /Frazer Cunningham 161; /Janeanne Gilchrist 112, 124; /Andy Komorowski 7 bottom left, 163 (pictures 5, 6, 10), 164 (pictures 1, 3, 4, 5, 6, 9, 11), 165 (pictures 1, 4, 5, 6, 7, 9, 11), 166 top left, 166 top right, 167 centre left, 167 centre right, 168 top centre, 168 centre, 168 top right, 168 bottom right, 169 top left, 169 centre right, 170 top centre, 171 top left, 171 centre, 171 bottom right, 172 (pictures 1, 3), 173 (pictures 3, 4, 5); /Lis Parsons 120 top right; /Mike Prior 110, 160; /Guy Ryecart 2 bottom left, 54, 119 top centre, 163 (pictures 1, 2, 3, 4, 7, 8, 9), 164 (pictures 2, 7, 8, 10, 12), 165 (pictures 2, 3, 8, 10, 12), 166 centre right, 167 top right, 168 centre left, 169 centre left, 169 bottom right, 169 bottom left, 170 centre left, 170 centre, 170 top right, 170 bottom right, 170 bottom left, 171 top right, 171 centre right, 171 bottom left, 172 (pictures 2, 4, 5), 173 (pictures 1, 2); /Peter Pugh-Cook 77; /George Wright 118. **Nasa/Jet Propulsion Laboratory** 52. **Photodisc** 49, 55, 108. **The Picture Desk Ltd.**/The Art Archive/Dagli Orti 41 bottom left.